Cardboard Wedding Cakes

Barry's Works, Kirkcaldy, which made shell casings during the war. Mrs Jean Fraser nee Roberts (whose wedding photograph is on the front cover) is in the back row, fourth from right.

Cardboard Wedding Cakes

the lives of the ordinary people of Fife
during the Second World War

Chris Neale

Fife Council – Community Services
Libraries
2005

Front cover: **Wedding of Alexander Fraser and Jean Roberts, 23 November 1940. (The bride's dress was made from parachute silk.)**

Published by
Fife Council – Community Services
Libraries

Fife
C O U N C I L
Community Services

Heritage Lottery Fund

Printed by
Cordfall Ltd
0141 572 0878

Preface

It is now sixty years since the end of the greatest conflict the world has known. The story of that clash of nations and armies across the seas and continents of the world has been told and retold many times. But, within that story, there is contained the stories of countless numbers of ordinary individuals. This book has been composed from the reminiscences of those who remember what it was like to lead their everyday lives in the shadow of great events.

In Fife, as elsewhere, life had to go on. The War was to bring separation to families, government directives would control almost every aspect of life, from shopping to leisure, work, and movement, and new duties and obligations were to be placed on every citizen. In the meantime a living had to be earned, families had to be fed, children had to be educated. History is, among other things, the story of families and communities. This book is about *our* families and *our* communities.

The Second World War now seems a long time ago. Most of those who can remember those momentous times are, sadly, no longer with us. But the consequences of that conflict still affect our lives and the society we live in. Everyone *thinks* they know about the War, if only from films and television documentaries, but historians (and common sense) tell us that only the people with first hand experience can know what it was *really* like. The staff of Fife Council Libraries are to be warmly congratulated on their initiative and enterprise in producing this work but, more importantly, our gratitude is owed to that generation of the people of Fife who have so generously shared their memories and their experiences with us.

John Simpson,
The Provost of Fife

Acknowledgements

Fife Council Libraries would like to thank the many individuals who have freely contributed their memories to our Home Front Recall Project.

We are grateful also to the proprietors of the following newspapers for permission to quote archival material: *The Dunfermline Press, The Dunfermline Journal, The Fife Free Press, The Courier,* and *The East Fife Mail.*

We would also like to express our gratitude to Natasha Keatch and Lisa Paterson of the Scottish Mining Museum for providing access to their oral history archive.

In addition to providing us with his reminiscences, Jim Douglas has given us permission to quote from his soon-to-be-published memoir of his childhood in 1940s Kelty, *Run to the Rainbow.*

The author would like to thank Eric Simpson who read this book in manuscript and who made a number of helpful suggestions. He is not, of course, responsible for any faults or errors which remain.

Finally, we must thank the Heritage Lottery Fund for the Award which has made this book possible.

Contents

CIVILIAN RESPIRATOR DRILL

Hold respirator by side of head-harness, dig chin into facepiece and draw straps over head by thumbs. See straps are not twisted. Always remove civilian respirator from the back, never from the front.

How to fit and wear the standard civilian issue gas mask.
From *The Complete First Aid Outfit and A.R.P.* A standard manual used by Wardens in Fife.

Introduction

On Sunday 3rd September 1939, at around quarter past eleven, the Rev W A Hutchison of St Andrew's South Church in Dunfermline rose to begin morning service as usual. But, instead of announcing the opening hymn, he informed the congregation that Britain and her allies were now at war with Germany. With almost theatrical timing his announcement was immediately followed by the soon-to-be familiar sound of the air raid siren. Most of his congregation duly filed into the public shelter under the offices of A & W Burt, Solicitors in Queen Anne Street. Similar scenes were being enacted in most of the towns and villages of Fife and, in fact, across the country.

The, by now long-awaited, conflict had begun. In Fife, as in other parts of Britain, many feared what they imagined lay ahead: aerial bombardment certainly, and the possibility of invasion. Some believed that Fife would be a priority target of enemy bombing. The coalfields and factories of west and central Fife were of obvious economic importance but, with more certainty, the Forth Estuary, with its dockyard and naval base, its bridges and shipyards, seemed likely to attract enemy attention. For more than a year, as the certainty of war loomed, the population had been prepared, both psychologically and physically, for the assault from the air. Gas masks had been issued, public shelters prepared, and air raid procedures put in place.

In Rosyth householders were issued with Anderson shelters. Civil Defence planners would have been impressed with the efficiency with which the Archbold family dealt with theirs. Mr Archbold was 12 years old when war broke out and lived with his mum and dad, two brothers and a sister. He has surprisingly clear and vivid memories of helping his father to erect the shelter:

> You had to dig out an area as detailed on the information sheet and as the water table where we resided was at 3 feet below ground level we could only dig to a depth of 2 feet 6 inches. The shelter consisted of 6 sections of corrugated sheet bent at the top to form the roof and joined together with 3 flat pieces of corrugated iron

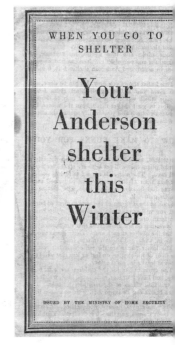

WHEN YOU GO TO SHELTER

Your Anderson shelter this Winter

ISSUED BY THE MINISTRY OF HOME SECURITY

One of the flood of public information leaflets which Government Ministries aimed at householders during the early stage of the war. Others included advice on cookery, preserving food, blackout procedures, growing your own vegetables, tobacco etc.

Nobody had any excuse for not knowing how to put on a gas mask. Here Fife factory workers rehearse each other in the procedure.

Mr Napier of Dunfermline displays the ideally constructed family shelter. Note the layer of soil packed carefully over the corrugated iron roof.

with front and back sections. We helped our father to dig out the ground to the size quoted in the information sheet and assembled the shelter as instructed bolting together all sections to form a strong unit. After [it was] assembled in the hole all the earth dug out was placed up the sides and over the top and covered with turf. My father made bunks on each side to accommodate 5 children and seats at the back for Mum and Dad.

The Archbold family shelter was never put to the ultimate test but I have no doubt that it would have passed the challenge.

In Lochgelly, Jim Clarke's father had even more ambition:

The embankment at the back of our gardens [which is now Benarty Avenue] was quite steep. A field at the top of the embankment stretched to Cooper ha'. Dad decided to build his own shelter and between my older brother and Dad we tunnelled into the embankment. I wheelbarrowed old bricks from the Lochgelly brickworks and when dumped took a hammer and chisel to chip off the cement. The Council supplied a bricklayer to build the shelter and put a reinforced concrete roof on it. All of the excavated soil was shovelled on to the top of the shelter. We then built a maze 6 foot high path to the shelter door. Dad's reasoning was a direct bomb wouldn't penetrate the shelter and the maze path would prevent shrapnel from striking the door ... Dad applied the skills he learned from working down the coalmines.

One of the first Anderson Shelters to be erected in Fife. The operation drew, as such spectacles do, an amused audience of small boys.

Advice to the population in the early months of the war regarding correct behaviour during air raids covered a wide range of scenarios. Here two Dunfermline carters (and their horses) demonstrate the appropriate response.

When an air raid warning sounds it is compulsory that horses be loosened from the traces and unyoked from the carts. The feed-bags must also be fixed on the horse. Here is a scene during Friday's warning.

Blackout conditions caused many accidents: some trivial but many were serious or fatal. A great deal of white paint was used to try to reduce risks.

In the general air of tension and uncertainty which prevailed in the early months of the war preparing to protect your family was an obvious course of action with immediate, practical benefits. Psychologically, too, it must have provided protection against the more vague, unsettling worries which disturbed those who projected their minds into an uncertain future. Ray Halford of Cupar remembers:

The Saturday before war broke out my mum and dad had saved up and bought a new wireless. And the first thing we heard on Sunday morning was the declaration of war. We lived in Westport Place at the top of the cul de sac and my aunt and my grannie came round and there was also my mum, my dad, my younger brother and myself. And my dad sent for my auntie Jean to come

14

More judicious use of white paint in an effort to maintain road safety during the blackout.

Among the many new restrictions that have been brought into force is one that compels motorists who travel by night to have their bumpers and running boards painted white. Here is the operation in progress by a West Fife car driver—

round with her box camera and take our picture so if anything happened to us during the war there was a recording of us.

And who could blame him? The next thing Ray has strong memories of was:

going to a house called Haymount which was on the corner of the Perth Road and we were all issued with gas masks in the cardboard boxes and the babies got the ones where you put the whole baby in and the mother pumped the handle so if anything happened to the mother then the baby had had it as well.

The issue of gas masks and the training in their use were sinister reminders to individuals of what might lay ahead. No one liked them. Jim Mackie had just started at Ballingry School:

The smell! They got very hot from the breathing. And every now and then the councillors would come in and see you doing your gas mask drill. But they never had theirs on!

And Fife's educational system, not previously known for its tolerant attitude towards classroom discipline, had discovered a new disciplinary offence. Although not guilty herself, Winifred Hislop remembered:

people getting the strap from the Headmaster for not bringing their gas mask to school.

If gas masks and air raid shelters were not enough to remind Fifers that 'there was a war on,' then the institution of the blackout made sure that, from sunset to dawn at least, the county was on a rigorous war footing. A force of Wardens was created who, along with Special Constables, ensured compliance with the regulations from the streets and tenements of the towns to the remotest farmhouse. Memories of this feature of wartime life remain keen. Jim Clarke, as a boy in Lochgelly, used to help the Warden on his patrol:

> I recall we went out at night to check the houses that were showing chinks of light. Every house had window frames made, and what was called tar paper was nailed on to the frames. We were given instructions to visit the elderly and secure their blackout window frames. We were also told when we saw a chink of light not to be afraid to tell them to be more careful. Moonlight nights were a bonus to allow us to manoeuvre. When the moon was hidden behind clouds it was inky black and next to impossible to see. We all carried sticks and used to rattle them against the walls to guide us home.

There must have been an eerie quality to moving around in such complete darkness, as David Mason admits:

> For me the blackout was strange. Once it was dark, that was it, if you were walking home it was easy to walk into a lamppost, or fall into a hole.

For George Docherty, who was only five years old, it was downright frightening. His earliest memory of all was: 'that it was dark, everywhere was very dark'. When he was staying at his grandmother's in Lochgelly's Happy Land, two of his uncles, who were miners, would walk him half the way home after school and then let him do the rest by himself. It was scary, pitch black, and he was shaking. He would run home as fast as he could. For others, it could be a bit of an adventure. Mollie Balfour remembers it as such:

> What excitement! To be out in the dark in my pyjamas and coat, meeting the other kids out in the middle of the night, no thought of danger . . .

And it could be dangerous enough as newspapers increasingly reported accidents and fatalities on the County's darkened roads. Mostly unreported were the numerous small mishaps that bedevilled the night-time traveller:

> It wasn't the first time I went to work with a black eye after walking

into a lamppost in the blackout.

Users of public transport fared no better. Margaret Joy remembers the:

> black blinds on each of the windows of the bus with only a small
> flap about six by four inches which the conductress would use to
> find out where the bus was . . . not always too successfully!

For James Melville the Kirkcaldy buses are not remembered with much
affection. They had:

> singularly uncomfortable wooden seats and interior lights
> completely covered by a shield that had only a very narrow slit to
> allow light to escape. In the resultant deep gloom there were many
> barked shins, scraped knees and torn stockings.

And what of the men who had to enforce this joyless regime, the ARP
Wardens? You get a sense sometimes that they were not universally loved.
Their job seemed, after all, to consist of checking on their neighbours
and issuing the peremptory command 'Put that light out!' Margaret
Green of Auchtermuchty recalls:

> The Warden went round and checked nobody was showing any
> lights because, if you were, they would blow the whistle and you
> got shouted at. He was always a black helmet. The ARP was a
> white helmet and he sat on the roofs watching for bombs falling.
> [His helmet made a lovely flowerpot after the war.] It was a cushy
> job; they used to sleep in the guide hall once a week.

But ARP Wardens had their trials too. Betty Mason's father used to say
it was always the same people who were careless – no matter how many
times they were told. And no doubt it was a provocation too far which
landed an East Fife Warden in Cupar's Sheriff Court. As the *Fife Free
Press* reported:

> Air-raid Warden, William Pryde, Ceres, near Cupar, assaulted a
> man whose attention he had drawn to a light on his premises. At
> Cupar sheriff court on Tuesday he was fined 40s. for striking
> Rolland Scott, hairdresser, Main Street, Ceres, on the mouth with
> his fist. His agent, Mr R D Gauld, solicitor, Cupar, told the Court
> that Pryde twice told Scott about a light, and Scott became abusive.
> Pryde became angry and struck him.

Curiously enough, beside all the relentless activities – such as those detailed above, as well as volunteer registration, ARP lectures, the requisitioning of premises for war work etc – there was also, at the war's beginning, a sudden closing down of some normal activities. School holidays, which were about to end, were extended. Cinemas and theatres closed. Many social and recreational organisations suspended their activity as if not quite sure whether it was appropriate for them to continue in their new circumstances. The professional league football programme was suspended and a severe limitation was placed on the attendances which were permitted to watch any friendly matches. Stadiums such as Dunfermline Athletic's East End Park were seen as resources which could be utilised for war purposes such as temporary

Air Raid Wardens at church parade in Townhill and also in a formal group portrait. (1940)

accommodation for military units. Fortunately not everyone succumbed to this tendency to shut down 'for the duration'. As the *Fife Free Press* reported on 16 September 1939:

> Leven Rotarians have decided not to discontinue their weekly club luncheons, as it is felt that in these anxious days there is greater need even than in time of peace for fellowship and social intercourse.

No doubt the Rotary Club enjoyed their lunch even more when they felt that they were contributing to the war effort and the maintenance of morale.

And, in fact, despite what looked at the beginning of the war like the beginnings of a total social paralysis, 'normal' activities were very soon resumed. A varied programme of regional football competitions with 'guest' players from forces units stationed locally proved highly popular. Cinemas reopened and, along with dancing, became an essential diversion for the population throughout the war years. Dunfermline's Opera House, after closing for two weeks, continued the run of Charlie Kemble and his Nu-optimists. The people of Fife could not be kept entertained by building air raid shelters and collecting salvage for long.

The adjustment of the population to wartime conditions continued alongside the preparation for the conflict itself. Anti aircraft gun emplacements and barrage balloon defences were installed along the Forth. Watching posts were located on Fife's North Sea coast. An anti tank trench was excavated across the County from Kirkcaldy to the Tay. Troop and naval deployments continued to increase. People were entitled to wonder what lay in store for them. Bomb and gas attacks on the civil

Overleaf: Advice for the 'stout-hearted citizen'. Be cheerful and of good courage. Use all of your powers to overcome the enemy. (But don't make 'independent attacks on military formations'.) Such action would be 'futile'.

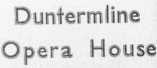

Variety thrived in wartime Dunfermline.

(d) West—

McLean School, Baldridgeburn. West gate pillars. (School is Rest Centre. Wardens' Post nearby).

Gate Pillars at Milesmark School (Wardens' Post).

Gate Pillars at Golfdrum Church (Church Hall is Emergency Mortuary).

Notice Board at Brown's Laundry, Grieve Street (Wardens' Post).

Public Shelter, south side of Pittencrieff Street, west of Glen entrance. (Wardens' Post nearby).

Sub Post Office at Chalmers Street, opposite Glen Bridge.

(e) Central—

City Police Office, Kirkgate.

Wall of City Chambers, Bridge Street frontage.

Notice Board, County Buildings, High Street.

G.P.O., Pilmuir Street.

Notice Boards at entrance to Carnegie Baths, Pilmuir Street (Emergency Hospital nearby).

Front wall of Fire Station, Carnegie Street.

Notice Board at Cinema, East Port.

Gate Pillars at Carnegie United Kingdom Trust Offices, New Row (Wardens' Post).

Front wall of A.R.P. Headquarters, Abbot Street.

Alexander's Hut at Bus Stance, St Margaret's Street.

II.—TOWNHILL—

Notice Board at new Police Station.

Gate Pillars, Carnegie Institute, Main Street (F.A.P.).

Brick Wall at junction of Kingseat Road and Townhill Road, Kingseathill.

III.—KINGSEAT—

Wardens' Post, Carnegie Institute, Kingseat (brick wall).

IV.—ROSYTH—

Palace Picture House, Queensferry Road (Wardens' Post nearby).

Notice Board at Police Station, Parkside Street, Rosyth.

Notice Board at new Police Station at junction of Admiralty Road and Queensferry Road.

Wardens' Post, Middlebank Street.

STAND FIRM.

RESIST THE ENEMY IN EVERY WAY POSSIBLE.

GIVE HIM NO ASSISTANCE OR INFORMATION.

DO EVERYTHING IN YOUR POWER TO AID OUR TROOPS AND CIVIL DEFENCE SERVICES.

BE CHEERFUL AND OF GOOD COURAGE AT ALL TIMES AND DEFEAT THE ENEMY'S AIM TO DEMORALISE AND TERRORISE THE CIVILIAN POPULATION.

Councillor WM. DICK, A.R.P. Joint Controller.

On behalf of the Civil Defence Committee of the City and Royal Burgh of Dunfermline.

" PRESS " OFFICE, DUNFERMLINE.

CITY AND ROYAL BURGH OF DUNFERMLINE.

NOTES FOR THE GUIDANCE OF THE PUBLIC DURING INVASION CONDITIONS.

Have you thought out in advance what you would do in Invasion? It is against the interest not only of your neighbours but the whole Country if you are not prepared and do not understand the part you will be required to play. There is no room for complacency. Invasion is a possibility and **you must be prepared now to face the grim conditions which might arise.**

If the enemy should invade this Country, he must be driven out or destroyed as speedily as possible. Consequently, the well-being of the civilian population must, while the enemy is being dealt with, be necessarily of secondary consideration. You have already been informed in Government Leaflets what to do in the event of Invasion. The primary duty of the population is undoubtedly that of rendering every possible assistance to our own Troops, either by carrying out their instructions or by denying and refusing information and assistance to the enemy. The public must not on any account take independent action to hamper or combat the enemy. Such action might have a prejudicial effect upon military plans and requirements.

You should at the earliest opportunity read the Government Leaflets which contain most vital and useful advice for the guidance of every Citizen.

"STAND FIRM"—this is of paramount importance, but it does not mean that the public should adopt an attitude of passive inactivity to the enemy. In fact, all citizens will welcome opportunity, if and when the time comes, of resisting and defeating the enemy.

There are many ways in which the civilian population will be able to assist in the defence of their homes and City, and the Town Council's Emergency Committee (comprising Council members, the Military, and Government Departments) ask you to give careful attention and consideration to the following points :—

I. STAND FIRM.—Maintain your normal life as long as possible. Except under definite orders, or in discharge of essential duties, **you must keep off the roads.**

You must stay in your homes—**Do not attempt to leave the City** for some supposedly safer area. The refugee movement which caused disaster in the Battle of France will not be allowed here.

II. CAN THE CIVILIAN FIGHT?—If stray enemy marauders or small parties of the enemy are moving about in any part of the City not in the effective occupation of the enemy, every stout-hearted citizen will be expected to use all of his powers to overcome them.

You must not, however, on any account, set out to make independent attacks on military formations of the enemy. Such action would probably be futile and actually impede the operations of our own troops.

III. EVACUATION.—Persons living near road blocks or any place required for military purposes, etc., may be asked, in their own interests, to remove from their homes. If you are ordered to do so, either by the Military or Civil Authorities, you should obey without question or delay.

All such citizens should make alternative arrangements to reside with friends not living in the vicinity of such road blocks, should the necessity arise.

MAKE SUCH ARRANGEMENTS NOW.

IV. CIVILIAN LABOUR.—The help of all able-bodied men and women may be required to fill in craters or remove debris from roads, dig trenches in waste ground, gardens, etc. Be ready and willing to give this help when called upon.

The call will be made at the time by loud speakers and also by notices posted on the official boards referred to in Paragraph 12. You will probably require to bring and use your own spade, shovel, or wheel-barrow. **Look them out now and see that they are easily available.**

Every able-bodied citizen will also be expected, if called upon, to assist with the creation and removal of road blocks. The Home Guard will ask you to help in this important work at the time.

V. WATER SUPPLIES.—Water is essential to the life of the Community— **It may well be scarce in Invasion. Do not waste water.** If water is contaminated you will be warned by loud speaker and official notices of that fact and of the action you should take.

Everything possible must be done in Invasion to conserve supplies of water. It may be necessary to order a reduction of consumption for domestic purposes. Citizens will be expected to honour such orders, and to carry them out faithfully.

VI. FOOD AND FUEL.—Restrict the consumption of food and fuel to the minimum—Give effect to official instructions regarding these. During periods of air raids, turn off the gas at the meter.

VII. RUMOUR.—There is nothing worse for morale than " Rumour." Do **not believe rumours and do not spread them.**

Any cases of Rumour coming to your notice should be immediately reported to the Police or Wardens by word of mouth only. **In doing so, please do not use the telephone or send written messages.**

VIII. AGRICULTURE.—The Government policy for food production in the event of invasion is for farmers to remain on their farms. **Stick to your jobs and go on producing food as long as possible.**

IX. HOMELESS PERSONS.—Invasion will probably be preceded by air attack. Rest Centres will be available. Homeless persons should immediately go to the house of their friends who have arranged to take them in or to their nearest Rest Centres. Remember the roads must be kept clear. If you are instructed to go to a billet, do so; don't start looking for your own accommodation unless you are quite sure of the address at which you will definitely get it. If you can live with friends or relatives, go there immediately. No attempt should be made to remove furniture and furnishings (except by consent of the Local Authority). You may take personal belongings. Use commonsense, and do nothing likely to hinder military operations.

X. CIVIL DEFENCE SERVICES.—Remember the Civil Defence Services will be operating in Invasion whether or not there is air attack. They will do all they can to assist you; but, like you, their primary duty will be to assist the military. The help therefore which can be given to you will be limited. Learn to become self-reliant. For example, can you administer first-aid, not only to your family, if need be, but to your neighbours? They may need your help. Such assistance will be valuable and appreciated.

XI. CIVIL ADMINISTRATION.—The Civil Authorities will, through their officials, maintain as well as circumstances permit, all essential services, but do not expect miracles. Such services will be maintained only as well as the situation and military needs permit.

XII. OFFICIAL INFORMATION.—Remember, only act upon authentic information. Such information will be displayed upon Official Notice Boards, supplemented where possible by loudspeaker vans, etc.

If you doubt the information in any way, enquire at your Warden, or at the Police. Provided you are satisfied as to the authenticity of instructions and orders, realise now that (if and when the times comes) you should immediately give effect to them. Don't argue about it—if you don't happen to agree—the persons issuing the orders and instructions will be in a better position than you to determine the necessity for issuing them.

DO NOT ACCEPT INSTRUCTIONS FROM STRANGERS.

Official notices will be displayed at the following points :—

I.—DUNFERMLINE

(a) North—
Sub Post Office, 59 Townhill Road—opposite Shamrock Street (blackout boards above doorway).
Wardens' Post, Arthur Street (brick wall).
Wardens' Post, "Oakbank," Rose Street (cement wall).
Sub Post Office, Campbell Street (dressed stone wall).

(b) South—
Gate Pillars at Priory Lane entrance to Queen Anne School (School Janitor nearby).
Wardens' Post at 52 Nethertown Broad Street.
Wardens' Post at corner of Mill Lane and St Leonard's Street.
Sub Post Office at junction of St Andrew's Street and Malcolm Street.
Wardens' Post at Aberdour Road.

(c) East—
Notice Boards at entrance to Public Park, Appin Crescent.
  Controlled by Wardens' Post at Carnegie Hall.
Transy entrance gates at junction Garvock Hill and Halbeath Road (Wardens' Post at 1 Halbeath Road).
Wardens' Post opposite Garvock Farm, Halbeath Road.
Gate Pillar at entrance to Touch Bleachfield (Wardens' Post).

population? Invasion and tank battles across the beet fields of East Fife?

At half past two on Monday 16 October 1939 it looked as if at least some of these fears might come to pass. The first air attack on Britain of the Second World War had begun. And it took place in the skies over the Forth Estuary. The military facts about the attack are fairly well established. It was a raid rather than one of the full scale attacks which became features of life in Britain's great population centres during the rest of the war. The Luftwaffe had the limited objective of damaging the naval shipping which lay at anchor in the Forth. Sixteen sailors were killed and forty-four were injured. Two German bombers were destroyed.

But what did the people who saw this action in the skies over their homes make of it? *The Dunfermline Press* later that week reported the event in these terms:

> The first intimation which Dunfermline received of the air raid was the sound of anti aircraft gunfire. As it had been impressed upon them for years that the civilian population would receive at least seven minutes' warning of an air raid most people were at first quite unconcerned and readily accepted the explanation that some sort of practice was in progress. It was an afternoon of brilliant sunshine, and hundreds of citizens stepped out of shops and offices to watch the puffs and rings of smoke where the anti aircraft shells were bursting at a great height.
>
> Gradually there came over the onlookers an uncomfortable feeling that what they were witnessing was no practice but the real thing . . . people in the Public Park actually heard the rattle of machine gun fire.

In North Queensferry, immediately below the action, housewives were hanging their washing out.

> They were startled by the rickety rackety noise made by the raiding planes, which came from the east and flew so low over the houses that the figures of the occupants of the machines and the Swastika emblem on the planes were clearly discernible. No bombs were dropped at that stage of the attack, but several articles of the drying clothes were afterwards found to be smeared with oil, which had evidently dropped from one of the bombers.

It is striking how many remember the event as a kind of spectacle, a free show. Ray O'Riordan recalls her family's experience:

> We lived in Queensferry and we lived in a house which is quite high above the river. And in September when the bombs came,

24

the German bombers came over and my mother and sister were both at home and they went out the front and, at the time, they had some maids and *they* were sent in so they didn't get bombed but Mother and Marjorie didn't want to miss the show. So they saw the German bombers coming in, they were not trying to bomb the Forth Bridge they were trying to bomb the ships below the Bridge, there were destroyers in front of us, across at South Queensferry, so they saw the bombs coming down, banging and splashing

And then ... that was it. The first serious air assault on Britain was more or less the last to affect the people of Fife in a direct way. What was feared would be merely the beginning of a prolonged offensive turned out to be a one-off. Fifers certainly experienced the extremes of military violence during the Second World War but, for the most part, that experience was gained elsewhere in service in more heavily targeted areas of the country and in every theatre of war overseas. At home, Hitler seemed to be ignoring Fife and, in fact, evolving military strategies meant that this would remain the case. The land campaign in Norway ended and, with it, the importance of the North Sea and the great naval base at Rosyth declined.

The convoy anchorage at Methil remained of importance and was an impressive sight. Mr Henderson remembered:

going down to the bottom of School Lane in Leven, looking across the Forth and feeling as if I could walk to the other side, there were so many boats. By noon it was clear.

But even this gathering received only sporadic attention from the enemy. For the most part the bombs that fell in Fife were the isolated result of aircraft shedding their bomb loads or occasional opportunistic forays by lone German raiders. Damage was minimal and casualties were few. The typical memories Fifers have of those incidents consist of hearing a loud bang or a series of explosions, then turning out the next day to inspect the damage. Jim Douglas recalls a few incendiary bombs falling in the Forestry Commission plantations near Kelty:

but then came the night of our biggest fright. We were huddled as usual in the shelter when the drone of a plane was heard overhead followed by the whistling of a bomb and a loud explosion. The house vibrated slightly and we crouched lower in fear. The whole village trooped out in the morning and in a field next to the Black Burn a great crater yawned. A cow and several sheep lay dead, their legs bent into unnatural positions. I gazed at the grotesque

corpses suitably impressed. Something that could kill an animal as large as a cow must be, indeed, dangerous.

But bombs, however isolated, could tragically affect individual families. As Mary Howie recalls:

> I lived in Cellardyke during the war. One Friday evening a neighbour asked me to run an errand to a small haberdashery shop in the village. When I was in the shop there was a loud bang and the shop shook, then the same thing happened a minute or so later ... we found out later that a house in Kilrenny had been directly hit with a bomb and the woman inside killed. Her son, who was in the garden at his rabbit hutch, was unharmed.

The bombing of Clydeside is recalled by many as Fife seemed to lie in the flight path. Mrs Hutchison remembers: 'the red glow in the sky the night of the Clydebank blitz' seen from over forty miles away. The memories of an eight-year-old include: 'when Glasgow was bombed we stood [she was with her Gran] on our outside landing and could see what was happening – in the distance'. Quite properly the memory doesn't linger over these matters:

> we in Cowdenbeath were very lucky, air raids but nothing to talk about. My grandmother cooked lovely meals despite rationing ... my favourite food was scrambled dried eggs and spam fritters!

And so the war years in Fife continued. It brought few great events but deep changes in the way people led their everyday lives. For the family and the individual nothing was quite as it had been before the War. From the mundane matter of what appeared on the dinner table to where people lived and worked, and with whom – not to mention the issue of whether they were given much choice. The following pages will try to describe some of these changes: as far as possible in the words and memories of Fifers themselves.

Opposite: **The Royal Observer Corps – trained in the tracking of enemy aircraft movements – gave sterling support to the anti-aircraft units of Scotland during the war. The pictures show the men of 36 group (Dunfermline).**

Ivor and Edwin Curran lie about their age in their attempt to join the army.

The Children's War

Perhaps surprisingly, the first memory of people who were children in Fife during the Second World War is a happy one. At the outbreak of war the authorities extended the summer holiday! Their motives were not to give children an extra few weeks' freedom to prepare themselves for any rigours ahead but were severely practical. Many school buildings had been pressed, partly or completely, into war service. Accommodation was under pressure and, to add to the difficulties, a major evacuation of children into, and across Fife, was under way.

It seems right to begin an account of children's experiences during the War with the topic of evacuation. Although only a minority of children was affected directly, the effects on the children and the families involved could be far-reaching and long-lived.

In Fife the evacuation of children and mothers from areas of perceived threat from bombing had been a concern of the local authority from early days and showed official planning at its best – and also, possibly, its worst. On 2 September 1939, the day before the declaration of war, 300 Edinburgh schoolchildren arrived in Dunfermline prior to being dispersed to destinations in West Fife. The Rosyth and Edinburgh areas had been identified as the areas most likely to be targeted by enemy bombing. When Rosyth children were lined up for evacuation they had already experienced a 'trial march' up to Rosyth Halt station: 'with our gas masks in a case around our shoulders and name-tags attached to us'. In the way of things not everyone had seen the need to *explain* to the children what was going on – or the need for it. Some memories of Edinburgh children, like those of Mrs Deans, make slightly uncomfortable reading:

> My memory is at the time we were staying at Warriston Place and we stayed at the basement flat. I had watched for two or three days this little black car making its way along Warrington Crescent and my friends disappearing into it, never to be seen again! I stood at the top of the stairs watching for this car coming to our house, and I was thinking to myself I'm not going away with a stranger,

Before the fateful news at 11 a.m. on Sunday, September 3rd, the children of Rosyth were moved to safety. The evacuation was carried out w hitch. Picture shows a group of the mothers and children before leaving Park Road School for the centre of Fife. Note the gas masks which hav a "vogue" in the area ―――――

A newspaper photograph of the Rosyth evacuees in September 1939. Most were home before Christmas.

never to come back again. When I did see it coming to our house I went down into the bathroom and locked the door and of course there were bars on the window which stopped them getting in to unlock the door. They shouted 'come on now, you're going to be evacuated,' and I shouted 'no I'm not going cos people don't come back'. . . . Oh I'll never forget that, watching this black car.

The official view of the Rosyth evacuation was that events had moved like clockwork, as expressed in the, slightly complacent, but still rather moving account published in the *Dunfermline Journal*. The piece was headlined, 'NOT A CHILD CRIED: NOT A PARENT CHEERED':

The evacuation of the children of Rosyth went off without a hitch last Saturday afternoon. From before 1.30 p.m. children, many of pre-school age, were finding their way to the schools, loaded with small cases of necessities and with gas masks slung over their shoulders. The children with the mothers who were also going were admitted to the schools at 2.00 p.m., and immediately began the formalities of registering, labelling and checking baggage. At 3.15 p.m. the buses arrived to take young children and mothers to the station, and at 3.30 all were assembled at the Halt station.
    King's Road School, which was the first to go, left at 3.45 p.m.

There were no 'scenes' as the train drew into the platform. Everyone stood still in his or her appointed place and were marshalled in turn into the empty coaches.

As the train drew out silence reigned. A few of the small crowd of anxious, dry-eyed mothers waved handkerchiefs. A lonely voice was heard to shout a last farewell and the first of the children passed out of the 'danger-zone'.

For most evacuees the experience was relatively brief. By Christmas 1939 over half of the 755 mothers and children who had left Rosyth had returned. And for some the experience was largely a positive one. Mr Archbold found that:

> the estate, Annfield, was huge so we had acres of land to play in. We were all enrolled into school in Cupar and we were given sixpence to spend every day so we all bought oystershell ice creams at lunchtime.

He remembers making a football out of old rags and 'the lady of the house' suggested to the Laird that he could provide them with a real ball. And he did. An oval ball! Credit to the boys who did not succumb to class pressure but continued to play the soccer game with the alien intrusion. The experience provided an enjoyable taste of rural life – snaring rabbits and helping out on a dairy farm, 'we also helped at the harvesting, stooking the hay for drying and building haystacks'.

Margaret Fotheringham, Mr Archbold's sister, also enjoyed life around the Annfield estate, despite a less than encouraging start:

The bureaucracy of modern war. Like all local authorities Dunfermline Town Council turned its attention to matters such as protecting children from poison gas.

Gas masks were unpleasant and uncomfortable to wear. Perhaps children felt this even more. This picture shows a Fife child getting used to wearing his. Fortunately the mask hides the little boy's facial expression.

> Mum had asked if at all possible we were not to be separated, but we were! The three boys got out and I was taken along the road to a cottage and left with a man and a woman. They showed me where my bedroom was, and helped to put all my clothes away, then had something to eat and the lady gave me a bath and put my nightclothes on. Then there was a knock at the door 'sorry we've delivered the wrong girl to you' . . . so back in the taxi to arrive at Cluny Cottage which was to be my home for the next year.

And where she was given the wholly unwelcome offer of another bath. (Bathed before she left Rosyth, this would have been her third bath of the day.) But, like her older brothers, she settled in well:

> After school [in Kingskettle] we used to go to Samson's farm and watch them making cream in the dairy, gather eggs, watch them

bring in the cows, play in the hayloft. I often think what great patience they had with us. I don't remember ever being told off by either the Samsons or the Givens.

Some children didn't feel so privileged. Robert Grant remembers:

evacuees being gathered in a school hall where they were chosen by villagers in a method resembling choosing a puppy or a kitten.

Sometimes there could be something of a cultural mismatch. Mrs Mylczynska was a patrol leader with the Girl Guides in Cupar:

Guides were asked to help take evacuees from Edinburgh to their new families. My dad helped by driving children to houses outwith Cupar. They were very particular about which houses evacuees were sent to. Some evacuees went to Kilmaron Castle but were very roughly brought up children who did not know how to conduct themselves in even the most basic of ways. Some of the Girl Guides were asked to go to Kilmaron to help look after these children.

Generally the evacuation of children in wartime was undertaken with the highest of motives. But it *was* a social experiment with not always very happy consequences:

We went to a church and people from Newport came to pick. We were three children and nobody wanted three children but because my mother was there, this elderly couple took us. My mother had

At Ballingry School, the headmaster's wife, Mrs Mackie, commandeered the playground (and the children) to plant vegetables.

to go home after six or seven weeks and that's when the trouble started – the elderly couple couldn't cope. I was eight, my brother was six and my sister was ten so then we were separated. The woman upstairs took my sister because she was older and she could help with the chores. The woman downstairs took my brother and me but she had two children and her own two kids had been evacuated and she said this wasn't fair and we would have to go somewhere else. We then went to a family who were really poor. I think the only reason they took us was to get money from the government. They had two daughters and one of them ill-treated my brother and me . . . Oh it was a terrible place.

Some children avoided evacuation at the last minute. Mrs Cowan remembers hearing her mother and grandmother talking about it:

. . . lovely long ringlets in my hair and my mother said I had to have it cut. So I took myself off to every barber's shop in Inverkeithing and they all refused and I said 'but I'm going to be evacuated and my mother said it wouldn't be looked after!' Eventually this barber cut it straight across and when I got home my mother burst into tears and said go and let your granny see it and she did the same. After that she wouldn't part with me and said, 'No, just stay at home!'

A few, very few really, took the ultimate step of sending their children to stay with relatives overseas. Ian and Andrew Herd were sent to stay with their uncle in Wonthaggi in Australia in August 1939. Homesickness appeared to be the least of the boys' problems as Ian wrote to his parents

From the beginning it was important that children should be seen as supporting the war effort. Comforts for the troops was one area where children could be enrolled. Here boys of Commercial School, Dunfermline display their knitting prowess (1940).

Girls from Dunfermline High School – rather self-consciously – are photographed knitting comforts for the troops.

MITTENS WITH FINGERS

THE RIGHT HAND

COMMENCE by casting on 64 stitches, 20 stitches on each of 2 needles and 24 stitches on the 3rd needle.

Work round and round in ribbing of knit 2 and purl 2 for 36 rounds or 3½ inches.

Now shape for the thumb gusset as follows :

Next round : Purl 1, knit into the front and back of the next 2 stitches, knit 1, purl 1, knit to end of round.

Next 2 rounds : Purl 1, knit 5, purl 1, knit to end of round.

Next round : Purl 1, knit into the front and back of the next stitch, knit 2, knit into the front and back of the next stitch, knit 1, purl 1, knit to end of round.

Next 2 rounds : Purl 1, knit 7, purl 1, knit to end of round.

Next round : Purl 1, knit into the front and back of the next stitch, knit 4, knit into the front and back of the next stitch, knit 1, purl 1, knit to end of round.

Next 2 rounds : Purl 1, knit 9, purl 1, knit to end of round.

Next round : Purl 1, knit into the front and back of the next stitch, knit 6, knit

B.W. No. 68

One way in which almost anybody could support the war effort was by knitting comforts for the troops. The illustration is from a magazine devoted solely to that activity: *Bestway War Knitting no 78.*

in a letter passed on to a local newspaper by his amused (and possibly bemused) parents.

Dear Mum and Dad

    I had a good trip out ... and it's great out at Uncle Dave's farm and a boy in our grade at school has a horse and he says I can ride it when I like all I have to do is go down to the paddock and get it ... so don't think you'll get me back when the war's finished. It's fine away up here in the bush. Andy's coming back but I am not so Goodbye

Your loving son
Ian

Although the above example is amusing the realities of separation from one or both parents were often disturbing. Mrs Curran of Kirkcaldy remembers her dad coming home on leave: 'It was just like a stranger coming into the house and taking over.' Margaret Garvie's father saw her for the second time (the first was when she was ten days old) when she was five. Her father looked through the kitchen window where Margaret and her cousins were playing: 'Which one's mine?' he had to ask. Jean Herd was about four when she first saw her dad. She was outside her grandmother's house when a man in army uniform picked her up in his arms. Later when he was asked how he had recognised his daughter he said that actually he had recognised her woollen jumper from the description given by his sister who had knitted it.

Evacuation was, of course, the expression of everyone's natural concern for children's safety. Much effort in schools was put into instructing and rehearsing children into the proper way to behave during an air raid. A ten-point plan was devised by a Rosyth schoolteacher and was widely distributed. Some of the points required rather complicated calculation by the children but most were sensible. (Some were plain daft.)

3. Find exactly the place where you are half way between the school and your home if you stay within ten minutes' walk of the school.
4. If you hear air-raid sirens on your way to school and you have not reached half way – run home (or to a public shelter if one is nearest)
   Never stop to look up at the sky even if you hear planes and gunfire – run to the nearest house and the lady will take you indoors.

The education authority never let slip the opportunity to enrol pupils in the war effort. Here, Dunfermline High School boys are digging up the school grounds for vegetable planting in 1940.

Note – if you ever forget what to do during an alarm, run to the nearest house and ask to be taken in.

Note to parents – if your child lives at a greater distance from the school than ten minutes' walk, find the two points on his route that are five minutes from either end . . .

Sometimes it seems that small boys were the chief beneficiaries of the War. John Corbett of Cupar was only five when war broke out:

but because all the men were away we went wild – I used to run away in the morning so Mum wouldn't give me jobs to do – had lots of fun.

Norman Cunningham of Leven recalls that:

Down the beach was super. The Polish Soldiers' mess hall was in the beach pavilion. Their cooks would give us a few potatoes which we roasted on the fire in the sand . . . the Polish Parachute Regiment was stationed at Largo House in Upper Largo. Four of us would sometimes walk along to Largo House to 'spy', to see what they were doing [mostly they were jumping through a hole in a barn roof onto bales of straw].

Youth organisations, especially the cadet groups in Fife's Secondary Schools, took on a rather military flavour as their task was seen as preparing young people for the spell of conscripted service which lay ahead. Here we see the Girls Training Corps on parade at Dunfermline High School in 1942.

John McWilliams was a small boy in Kirkcaldy at the end of the war and remembers German Prisoners of War being transported along his street (Front Lebanon) on the way to the Council depot. One day, as snow lay on the ground, John and his gang decided to ambush the convoy and:

we had great fun throwing snowballs into the back of the trucks. To our minds the Germans were well and truly beaten but we made the mistake of following the lorries into the depot.

The POWs piled out of the trucks and began to return the gang's fire with interest: 'then we knew what being beaten was all about'.

For the budding anorak there were the local branches of the National Association of Spotters' Clubs. Bert McEwan remembers the one organised in the Children's Department of Dunfermline's Central library. Using a home-made epidiascope, the Children's Librarian, Miss Whyte, used to flash silhouettes of the tailfins or fuselages of Heinkels and Messerschmitts on to a screen while boys – I think it was always boys – would demonstrate their Aircraft Recognition skills. Youth organisations in the schools increasingly were represented by those who offered a practical training to prepare for future adult service. May Edmondson of Kirkcaldy remembers:

> I was in the Girls' Training Corps, it met in the gym at the High School and you did things like drill, signalling, aircraft recognition, and First Aid. Everyone wore their own navy skirt and cardigan and a white blouse. And there was a forage cap with a badge.

As usual, the more interesting activities were reserved for the boys:

> The boys used to play 'fighting the Germans'. They wanted to be the British. The girls got a game if they would be Germans.

Both Bert McEwan and David Mason were in their respective school Air Training Corps at Dunfermline and Cowdenbeath. Both enjoyed air trips in elderly, Swordfish open-cockpit biplanes, while David experienced a flight on a flying boat ending with a hair-raising (to him) landing on the Tay.

It would be wrong to suggest that children were always passive observers of the various war-related activities by which they were surrounded. Many were involved in the constant fund raising that went on in Fife towns and villages at that time:

'CHILDREN'S WAR EFFORT' was the headline of an article in the *Fife Free Press* on 11 September 1943.

> The kiddies of Viceroy Street are doing their bit towards the lads and lasses of this street who are now in uniform by running a series of concerts, whist drives, etc., in an effort to raise money in order to send a Xmas gift to each. The first of these series was in the form of a 'Back Yard Concert,' held on Monday and Wednesday evenings, when the children gave a delightful performance, which included songs, dances, and recitations . . . to date the amount realised is £9 5s 4d.

Air Training Corps 792 Squadron, Dunfermline High School.

Air Training Corps 792 Squadron, Dunfermline High School, under inspection 1942.

Note the patronising 'kiddies'.

Although little effort was put into giving children a wider knowledge of the war: 'sometimes in geography you were shown where the fighting was on a map', and many were silenced into respectful attention while the nine o'clock news was listened to on the wireless, there were no qualms about using the children's efforts for the benefit of the community. *Beath High School Magazine* in 1944 reported their plans for the coming session:

> Later in the year these classes [IV, V and VI] will have five weeks of abstention from school, during which the services of our young people in the potato field will be required. The purpose of the broken holidays is to enable our pupils to play their full part in gathering in the grain and potato crops. Last year the response of the school was magnificent, and we are quite convinced that the patriotism which shone so brightly last year will again be evinced in this time of our national need . . .
>
> Not only has the school played its part in the harvest field but on the occasions when intensive local effort is made the school plays a very active part in these good deeds. During the 'Salute the Soldier' campaign week, for example, it raised the sum of £1,271 15s.

But children remained essentially children: two charming contemporary documents reveal what children were really thinking about during the war. The first is the diary kept by the 'Poppy Patrol' of the 7th Dunfermline Girl Guides during the middle years of the war.

Salvage again. This time recruiting youth organisations in Dunfermline to collect paper. (1940)

May 3rd 1943 – All patrol here except for Sheila. Sheila was coming back but her mother was ill, marks won for games, attendance and punctuality. It has been decided that we shall give £5 to the Prisoners of War fund and the rest to the BP [Baden Powell]. There has to be a Youth Rally on May 16th and on May 12th all guides have to go to the High School playground for Company Drill by a Home Guard Sergeant.

October 25th Hallowe'en Party tonight. Everyone was ducking for apples and trying to bite a piece of treacle scone. We ended by eating mashed potatoes. Jean was one of the people who found a lucky charm.

The second document is a daily diary kept by Alex Cairns during the latter part of the war when he was a schoolboy in Kirkcaldy:

Sunday 6th February 1944
    Got out of bed at 10.05
    Had a real egg
    Cold and dull. Tommy Handley 12.30, Jack Benny 1.15,
        Happidrome 7.15

Some youth organisations continued their traditional activities. The Poppy Patrol diary of the 7th Dunfermline Girl Guides is a charming record of badge work, camps and other activities – mostly unrelated to the war concerns that could pervade every aspect of life, even for children.

Monday 6th March 1944
> Fine weather. Mild
> Got a French Test, English homework. Got Rugby today
> 2lb of butter came from New Zealand

Monday 7th May 1945
> Dull, not bad. Got a history test which we finished off at home
> Had a real egg
> Got results of arithmetic test (78%)
> War is finished: VE Day is not declared

Friday 10th August 1945
> Atomic Bombs 65% JAP SURRENDER
> Sunny, fine
> In the forenoon played with James and John at croquet
> Mum went to town in the afternoon and bought me sandshoes
> Dad and I put axles on trolley

Our memories of what life was like when we were children are often keenest. Honest, unsentimental memories of what it felt like to be a child during the War seem to give us a route to the past unavailable to us in any other way. What seems important to the child could never be guessed by the adult outsider. Adult memories are (quite often) edited and arranged in order of importance. Our childhood memories don't seem to go through the same process. Ruth Brown of Kirkcaldy was five when war broke out. With her parents she remembers travelling in London on the top of a bus and seeing the devastation in the streets caused by bombing. Coming home and travelling over the Forth Bridge the air raid siren went off and the train stopped. There was a long and tense silence. She doesn't remember being afraid but she remembers the waiter (it was the restaurant car) removing her soup well before she had finished it.

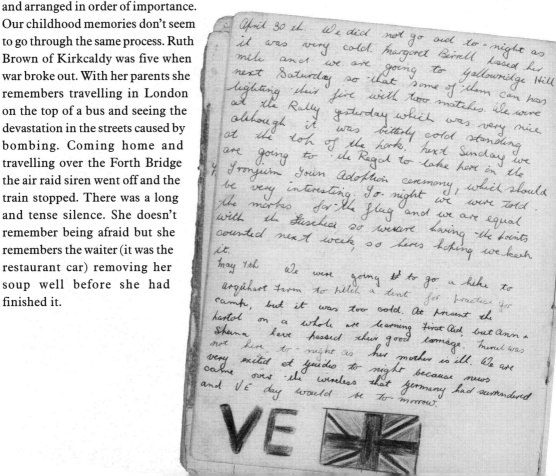

L236

MINISTRY OF FOOD

CHILD'S
Ration Book

OFFICIAL
PAID

CHILD'S NAME AND REGISTERED ADDRESS

Compare these
details with the
Child's Identity
Card and report
any difference to
the Local Food
Office

DO NOT ALTER

ISSUED
JULY 1942

If found return to

120 STE...
COWDENBEATH

FOOD OFFICE

Surname......Swanson

Other Names ....James

Address....17, Woodend Pl.,

Cowdenbeath

NAT. REG. No.	S 424	1940	140

SERIAL NUMBER OF BOOK

C 5 E 856100

R.B.2
5 (CH...

Eggs are not the only Food

Rationing, shortages, the black market, make-do-and-mend, queuing, wartime recipes for eggless cakes: we've all heard the stories from our parents and grandparents. What *was* all the fuss about? No one seems to have starved. Why do people of that generation all have memories of what rationing restrictions meant to them as individuals?

The first thing to say is that most people seem to have accepted that the *system* was fair. Jim Mackie of Lochore puts it very well:

> When you got your ration book everyone was the same. The allocation for everybody was the same. I mean you couldn't see that somebody was getting any more than you. Maybe you thought that some were getting more than you (maybe having friends working in the co-op) but the thing behind it was everybody was the same. We knew that. And you just had to get on with it.

But, of course, that was only the beginning of the matter. In order to be scrupulously fair the system was really a mass of (ever changing) regulations. In an area of life – feeding yourself and your family – which was once simply your own private business, you could now find yourself quite easily on the wrong side of the law (in August 1941 a labourer in Rosyth Dockyard was fined £7 with an alternative of 30 days' imprisonment for the crime of resetting a tin of gooseberry jam and a tin of orange marmalade) or, on the supply side, you might find yourself under pressure from customers to bend the rule. An egg or a child's bag of sweeties could be a can of worms! In fact most people seem to have made their own accommodation with the rules. If your granny had a hen farm and there was an extra egg to be had, so be it. With a family to feed, you could hardly think of yourself as a criminal if you took the chance to supplement the dinner table when the opportunity presented itself.

Opposite: The ration book: probably the most familiar document of all to the general population – during the war years and beyond.

Summer bargains must not be misconstrued on this picture. They actually mean dark blinds which cover you windows so that marauding airman will pass by. Women queued up at a Dunfermline shop this week to obtain yard or two from the thousands of yards

1939 and the newspapers reported the beginning of queues. At this time there were unlikely to be any major shortages but the Dunfermline shoppers in the picture were no doubt anticipating what lay ahead.

Jim Mackie again:

but I mean we were fortunate because up Benarty Hill and round about Ballingry we were polluted with rabbits and there were always plenty of poachers and they went round the rows selling them sixpence a pair – so you had boiled rabbit, fried rabbit, stewed rabbit, they even put it in the soup!

It would seem very hard to grudge Jim his rabbits – especially as he doesn't seem to have cared for them very much. May Edmondson's mother used a family connection to obtain hers:

An uncle of ours was a gamekeeper in Blairgowrie, and he'd sometimes send us a rabbit. It was wrapped in a newspaper and put on the bus. Mum and Dad would collect it at the bus station. Mum cured the skins after the rabbit was eaten and made linings for gloves.

Another effect of wartime rationing was the creation of a 'luxury' from what had once been a commonplace food item. This was certainly the case with the humble egg. Alex Cairns, in his schoolboy's diary repeatedly uses the phrase *a real egg*. No longer meaningful nowadays, this was an instantly recognisable term (along with *a shell egg*) which served to distinguish the real thing from its wartime substitute *powdered* egg. A real egg could be prized. Literally so in the case of Lorna Hunter's mum who:

> was a young girl during the war and at school she won two fresh eggs in a reading competition. The teacher had to escort her home with them to make sure they got home safely.

Janet Harper of Auchtermuchty must have been Fife's queen of eggs:

> We weren't too bad because my dad used to work on the farms, he was a slater and plasterer to trade and he used to get sent up to Sir John Gilmour's estate and of course Sir John used to say to him, just pick up any eggs you see lying around. We had cupboards full of eggs, everyone else was getting one a fortnight. My mother would have been arrested if it had been found out. You can say about it now, but you couldn't then.

But Janet's mother was by no means alone. Una White of Kirkcaldy remembers that her grandmother's cousin had a farm near Kingskettle:

> We used to come home with dozens of eggs which were plunged in isinglass and packed in a box so that they would last until next visit.

In households where there were no unofficial sources a scrupulous allocation could be enforced. May Jakonski recalls:

> I always remember there were eight of us in our house. One week four got a shell and four got powdered egg. When it was my turn for shell I would ask if I could have powdered egg instead. The stern reply was 'No!'

For this luxury, this most coveted prize among foods was not loved by all. Many came to *prefer* the powdered version. Irene May of Rosyth wishes you could get it now.

Next to eggs in importance seems to have come sugar and sweets. The sweet-toothed have memories of war as a constant craving. And not only the children. Ray Halford of Cupar remembers:

> My mother had a very sweet tooth and she loved sweeties and we went where the Courier office is now, it was a wee shop and it had

wee twin ladies in there, and so alike you couldn't tell them apart, the Misses Haig. We went there for our sweeties and our chocolate and there was one day she served some Polish soldiers their chocolate and when my mother's turn came it was, oh no, it's all finished and my mother was a gentle wee soul and she absolutely blew her top and we got chocolate from below the counter.

To avoid bloodshed, in the streets of Cupar as well as other Fife towns, many shopkeepers found themselves making their own 'adjustment' to the rationing system. May Jakonski again:

It was coupons for sweets, there was a wee shop beside us and they let us 'buy ahead'. I was never out of his shop and was months ahead of my ration. He used to say, 'you're going to land me in jail'. He was a good man!

He may well have been a good man but his fears were not entirely unfounded. Shopkeepers could be – and were – subject to court action when investigation uncovered discrepancies in their records. An Inverkeithing shopkeeper was found guilty of 'making reckless statements to the Fife County Food Committee' in 1943 and his case was reported in the local newspaper:

The fiscal said on each of the eight occasions accused had put in declarations of the numbers of coupons that were continually wrong. Over a period of eight weeks he declared that he had sent in 16,222 coupons, whereas the actual number he had sent in was 15,131.

The shopkeeper offered what was a common explanation:

With staff difficulties, and so many things to do in connection with food, an employer was often overcome with a sense of bewilderment and impotency. He attributed the mistakes made to the errors of unskilled and sometimes incapable assistants.

Bewildered and impotent or not, the defence was not allowed and a fine imposed.

Not much sympathy was felt for shopkeepers who, in addition to the official rationing scheme, often restricted supplies of some unrationed items to their regular customers. In fact they probably deserved a little more sympathy standing, as they did, between the Food Authorities, for whom they acted as unpaid administrators, and the customer who, quite reasonably, saw only their own need. Not all customers were scrupulous in their dealings with the system. Jane Elder worked in East Wemyss Co-op where she remembered some 'customers trying to rub out the marks the staff put on the cards'.

More important sometimes, than the dealings with the sources of supply, were the delicate negotiations that went on within families. In Margaret Green's family in Auchtermuchty: 'dad did a deal with us, he got the butter and the top of the milk and we got the sweetie ration'. In Jean McCallum's family in Wemyss:

> Mother got all the butter, Father (a miner) got marge. The sugar was put out in four bowls for each member of the family.

In one family, which perhaps ought not to be named, the father had been used to taking a piece to his work at the pit consisting of sugar on bread and butter. When war conditions threatened this preference he promptly allocated to himself the entire family ration of sugar and butter!

There were always temptations. When Jim Mackie and his fellow army cadets were employed to manhandle boxes of emergency supplies into the manse of Ballingry Church they could not help but notice that the packages were labelled BISCUITS. There seemed to be dozens of them. More temptation than hungry boys could reasonably be expected to resist. There was a surreptitious opening of the side of a carton and a quick grab of a handful of the contents. If Jim and his pals had delicious dreams of bourbons and custard creams they soon had cold water poured on them. The 'biscuits' were hard tack, the notorious hard-baked flour and water slabs which the Royal Navy had used as sea rations for centuries. Requiring soaking in soup or gravy to make them edible at all the first cadet experimenter (who was Jim) nearly lost his front teeth.

It is very interesting to hear how many people remember their wartime meals with relish. Norman Cunningham of Leven remembers:

> We, as a family, never went hungry. For breakfast I liked white bread 'saps', sometimes with sugar and a drink of water. For dinner [around noon] my choice was a huge plate of chappit tatties. Tea was lovely when dried egg was available!

As an evacuee Margaret Fotheringham stayed with the Givens family. Mr Givens was a baker with Kingskettle Co-op:

> At the weekend our treat was cakes. I loved the cornet shaped cakes with cream and jam. We had to eat bread, then a scone, then a cake. I tried to skip the scone to get my favourite cake only to have my fingers rapped, 'you haven't eaten your scone,' and, by the time I had eaten my scone the cake was gone!

Most of us will, at some time, have shared Margaret's anguish.

Jim Clarke, as a boy in a family of twelve:

> did most of the shopping at the Co-op in Minto Street [in Lochgelly]. The butcher always put a couple of ham bones in without charging. Mum's pea soup made with those bones was so tasty.

Of course some had responsibility for providing on a larger scale. The Elie Communal Kitchen was set up to provide catering for the small town's population of evacuees. The organisers were rather pleased to be noted in the November 1939 issue of the *Lancet*:

> In our little town in Fife the war has forced us to conduct an interesting dietetic experiment. We set up a communal kitchen for the evacuees; our treasurer was allowed to collect the 8s 6d a week for each child from the Post Office. He then handed over 3s per week to each householder and kept 5s 6d for the kitchen fund. The children get three meals a day at the kitchen and, much to our surprise, we find it can be done quite satisfactorily on this

Rationing, with its system of points, books, cancellations and registered traders, was complex and bureaucratic. Tolerated by the population perhaps because of its perceived fairness. Here a Dunfermline shopkeeper helps a young housewife get to grips with the system. (Or, perhaps, the other way round.)

sum. The mothers with children who feed at the kitchen have to pay for their own and their children's meals at the rate of 7s per week for adults, 5s 3d for children from 4 to 14 years, 3s 6d for children from 1 to 3 years and 1s 9d for children of less than 1 year.

For breakfast they had porridge and milk, tea, cocoa, and bread and butter. On Sundays they have eggs and fried bread. For midday dinners there are two meatless days with lentil or potato soup with brown bread and a suet pudding. On other days there are vegetable soup, and mince, stew, stoved potatoes, or shepherd's pie in turn. When there is no soup they get a pudding: bread pudding, fresh fruit and custard, pastry or sponge. On Sundays they have cold mince mould and fruit salad. Tea consists of tea and milk, bread, butter or jam, or buns, biscuits and on meatless days an apple or a piece of cheese extra.

Fortunately, most evacuees returned to their own homes after a few months – certainly adequately nourished – but surely longing for some home cooking, and desperate to forget that such things as 'cold mince mould' ever had existed.

Many foods were not rationed. Mrs Milczynska remembers the universally despised wartime sausage:

They were a bit of a joke – containing a tiny portion of actual meat and a huge amount of fat and crumbs – they all but disappeared in the frying pan.

Her family liked to maintain standards:

There may have been only margarine on the tea table but it was in a pretty butter dish.

It was possible during the War to eat 'off the ration' if you ate out. In London this could include dining at the Ritz. In Fife it was more likely to be a visit to the chip shop. In 1942 the range of eating out establishments was extended by the creation of the institutions known as British Restaurants. Most local authorities took advantage of the opportunity to become restaurateurs. In Dunfermline the Community Feeding Committee of the Town Council opened their 'Communal Feeding Enterprise' in converted shop premises in the High Street. Thankfully, it was quickly decided to name the facility 'The Queen's Restaurant', although there is, in fact, no record of any royal patronage. The Provost and his wife as well other members of the Town Council duly launched the restaurant in April 1942 with a special lunch, blessed by the Reverend Dollar of Dunfermline Abbey. William Watson, MP congratulated the Town Council:

> We are certainly embarking on enterprises which we never contemplated before this war started . . . there might be a great future for British Restaurants after the rationing system ceased . . . women were not only voluntarily going into industry, but were being compelled to go into industry, even married women who had household duties to perform. A British Restaurant would fulfil a very useful purpose where the woman of the house had not the time to cook a proper meal, and where a husband who was left to provide for himself might be assured of a well-cooked meal.

In fact, the restaurant opened every weekday between 12 and 2 p.m. and offered a very popular service. Its prices: tuppence ha'penny for soup, meat course for sevenpence, sweet for tuppence ha'penny, and tea for a penny were well within the means of working men and women.

For some families a parcel from overseas made all the difference. Una White's mother's cousin in Canada used to send food parcels:

> Mackintosh Red apples, tinned meat, venison (once). On one of my birthdays I got a box of Hershey bars – one for each pupil in my class. I had never before had my own whole bar of chocolate.

Or ever been so popular with her classmates perhaps. When Mrs Milczynska's mother mentioned in a letter to her sister in Washington that the quality of flour was very poor and she could not make a good cake with it:

> Auntie, amidst all the goodies in America thought we were starving so she started sending food parcels in which she always included beautifully white flour. It came in small linen bags which she used to unstitch and hide nylon stockings in the flour.

Ina McIntosh's husband was stationed in Algiers where there were orange groves:

> He used to pick them when they were still green and pack them into a little balsawood box. This was sent to me in Lochgelly. Nine oranges could be packed inside; however there tended only to be eight. Before nailing the top down the box had to be checked and censored by an officer and then stamped. My husband would have a tin of fifty cigarettes inside his shirt and that would replace one of the oranges as the box was being nailed closed. By the time

it arrived at my house some of the oranges would be ready to eat, and my dad was more than happy to see the wee tin of cigarettes. On the evening after that box arrived I was my father's pet!

Because it was not only foodstuffs that could sometimes be scarce. Annie Newey worked in a newsagent's in Kirkcaldy where cigarettes could be in short supply: 'the men used to watch for the station lorries delivering the big boxes they came in'. The rationing of clothing was felt keenly. Many remember being measured at school because clothing coupons were allocated on the basis of a child's size. When Margaret Green was in class 2 in secondary school she remembers:

> Everybody was told if you took a size three in shoes you were going to get extra coupons and I was one and a half and I remember the teacher put her foot behind mine and pushed it forward to make sure I got the extra coupons like everybody else. We got 14 extra coupons which was really quite a lot.

In Lochgelly Isabella Dryburgh's parents made sure there was no mistake:

> At school you got your feet measured. If your toe went over the line you got extra coupons. I was told to get my toe over the line!

Hand-me-downs and make-do-and-mend were the order of the day. According to Jim Clarke:

> Gender had no status in our house the boys were taught to sew and darn socks. When we wore a hole in the soles of our shoes and it wasn't our turn for new shoes, we cut a piece of cardboard inserted it in the shoe – and that became the sole of your shoe!

Ray Halford got all her auntie's hand-me-downs. At the end of the war when she was fourteen and starting work her aunt sent her, from Glasgow:

> this pair of nylon stockings, with seams up the back. They lasted for ages and I was the only one in Cupar with nylon stockings. I was the girl with nylon stockings. They didn't realise I only had the one pair.

She was one up on Esther Renfrew who remembers the well-known wartime expedient of painting her legs and the drawing of a black line up the back. Esther also recalls:

A less than convincing advertisement for the wartime garment which, though it had its fans, people were glad to cast aside at the end of the war.

using sugar and water to help set her hair in a Marcel wave which was fastened with kirby grips and then slept on that night to be set up for the next day.

Her mother used to take the cotton bags that flour came in and make them into hankies for Sunday and pillowcases.

Janet Harper became almost speechless when she remembered a less happy improvisation with flour bags:

> Clothing was another . . . I'll never forget the injustice of . . . my dad worked at Reedie's the baker's at Leven and he came home with a load of flour bags and my mother made them into knickers. And one of the pairs she made me had FLOUR printed across the bum. Oh I was mortified. I was eleven years old by then and all you got was 'can't be helped, you've got to have them'. But that was the biggest upset in my life, having to go to school with FLOUR written on my knickers . . . but you can laugh about it now.

War-time weddings, for some reason, often brought out the best in people: a willingness to share, and help your neighbour or relative. Cecilia Bennett of Kelty had many people to be thankful to:

> I got married during the war and my auntie made my wedding cake – it was sugar from one neighbour and butter from another and they helped put the cake together.

A lot of the old men, who had little need of their clothing coupons, gave them to her so she could acquire towels, sheets etc.

At least Cecilia got her cake! Some improvisations were more poignant. Chrissie Scott was married in 1944:

> Rationing made it more difficult having a proper wedding cake. I remember trying to cut the wedding cake, forgetting it was cardboard! We just had a wee sponge cake inside this cardboard casing, which looked like a cake covered with icing. The cardboard shape went back to the shop on the Monday.

Opposite: **British Restaurants were a popular innovation in the mid years of the war. A basic meal and no-frills service for less than a shilling was the aim. As 'eating out' was not on the ration a midday meal at one of Fife's municipal 'feeding centres' was more attractive than it sounds. This picture shows the behind the scenes operation at Inverkeithing's 'Civic'.**

Rina Pringle shows off her smart new Land Army uniform in her parents' living room in Cowdenbeath.

The Working Day – and Beyond

The ordinary people of Fife have always worked hard. The traditional occupations of weaving, mining, fishing, and farming created a tradition and culture where work was central to the identity of the individual and the community. And lack of it could be devastating to both. The coming of war did not change that. What it brought were new pressures and motivation. Work had been necessary to pay the rent and put food on the table. Now work became a patriotic and social duty. Warfare in the twentieth century was economic and production had to be maintained. And there were new communal responsibilities: fire-watching, civil defence, fund-raising, the billeting of evacuees, salvage. A voluntary effort was required. From everybody: from women and from children too.

Salvage efforts included the collection of cooking utensils. One Fife woman recalls handing in all her ashets 'since there was never anything worthwhile to cook in them'. The photograph shows volunteers collecting in Pilmuir street, Dunfermline. The actual value to the war effort of these metal salvage schemes has been questioned but they nevertheless gave individuals the feeling that they were contributing in a very practical way.

THIS

LOG BOOK

which will record the operational activities
of an Aircraft
is a tribute to the success achieved by

LOCHGELLY

SAVINGS COMMITTEE

in the

WINGS FOR VICTORY

NATIONAL SAVINGS CAMPAIGN · 1943

Target :- £ 20,000.
Achievement :- £ 51,842 : 16 : 10
also £1510 Free Gift for purchase of Parachutes
and Dinghies.
REPRESENTING
THE COST OF
2 MOSQUITOES.
2 SPITFIRES.

The 'Wings for Victory' campaign hit on the idea of communities 'purchasing' an aircraft with their fundraising. At the end of the aircraft's tour of duty the town or parish would be presented with that plane's logbook. Sometimes this would have a rather poignant effect as the logbook's final entry might read 'failed to return' or something of that nature.

AIRCRAFT
LOG BOOK

TYPE
Mosquito II

NUMBER
DZ 739

DESCRIPTION   Twin engined, mid-wing monoplane.
Single fin and rudder.

ARMAMENT
4 x 20 mm. Hispano guns
4 x .303" Browning guns

SQUADRON No.
456

THE CREW   Captain.
W/O Ratcliffe
F/O Mills

Wt. 12056/3405 4M 5/43 KJL/5024 Gp. 698/3

For 'War Weapons Week' in 1940 a captured German fighter plane was exhibited in front of the gates of Dunfermline's Pittencrieff Park.

Let Your Money "Fly"

LEVEN
"Wings for Victory" Week
JUNE 5th to 12th, 1943

Our Target---10 Fighters £50,000
"Fight for our Fighters"

In the Tunisian Victory the army was ably assisted by the R.A.F. You can help in the final assault on Germany by contributing every penny you can spare to the "Wings for Victory" Campaign. Let your savings fly over Berlin in the form of Bombers.

WILLIAM GERRETT, Provost.

LET YOUR MONEY "FLY"
(Winning Slogan by Miss JEAN LAUDER, The Craig, Adamson Terrace, Leven.)

WINGS FOR VICTORY

Programme   Threepence
Keep this Numbered Programme. It may be a Winner!

Let Your Money "Fly"

'SALUTE THE SOLDIER' WEEK

WHIST DRIVE & DANCE
(ORGANISED BY MRS W. H. NAIRN)
IN
CALEDONIAN HOTEL, LEVEN

THURSDAY, 15th JUNE, 1944.
Whist commences 6.45 prompt.   Dance, 10.15

WHIST TICKET   -   -   3s

LEVEN "WINGS FOR VICTORY" WEEK

WHIST DRIVE
(Organised by Mrs W. H. Nairn)
IN
CALEDONIAN HOTEL, LEVEN
ON
THURSDAY, 10th JUNE,
At 7 p.m. prompt

TICKET   -   -   2s 6d

Turn your L.S.D. into H.M.S.

LEVEN WARSHIP WEEK
APRIL 18th to 25th, 1942.

The Signal is SAVE.   What is your Answer?

Remember Nelson's famous signal which spelt Victory. Now, Leven, follow this signal and the result will spell the same—VICTORY.

SAVE, SAVE and SAVE is the SIGNAL.

WM. H. NAIRN, Provost.

"Turn your L.S.D. into H.M.S."
(Winning Slogan by JAMES BRUCE, 24 Letham Terrace, 14 years of age)

SELLING CENTRES
ALL BANKS—Monday to Friday,   10 a.m. to 3 p.m.
Saturday,   10 a.m. to 12 noon
POST OFFICE   8.30 a.m. to 6.30 p.m.
KIRKCALDY & DISTRICT TRUSTEE
SAVINGS BANK—Daily
Thursday and Saturday   10 a.m. to 4 p.m.
Monday, Tuesday, Thursday and   10 a.m. to 1 p.m.
Friday, Evening,
Wednesday and Saturday, Evening,   6 p.m. to 7 p.m.
Drill Hall—Monday to Saturday   6 p.m. to 8 p.m.
                                      6 p.m. to 9 p.m.

Programme   Twopence
Keep this Numbered Programme.   It may be a Winner!

Turn your L.S.D. into H.M.S.

Hasten the End by what you Lend

LEVEN
'SALUTE THE SOLDIER'
WEEK : 10th to 17th JUNE, 1944.

BY your splendid response during "Wings for Victory" Week you assisted in devastating Berlin—the nerve centre of Germany.

Now "Salute the Soldier" by putting up record savings so that in the final onslaught he will be well equipped for a speedy and decisive Victory.

WILLIAM GERRETT, Provost.

Programme
Price
Twopence

SALUTE THE SOLDIER

Keep this Numbered Programme It may be a Winner!

SPECIAL EVENTS ALL WEEK
ARMY & ARTS & CRAFTS EXHIBITIONS

Hasten the End by what you Lend

Fund raising was a permanent feature of civilian life during the war. As production rose and wages increased more ways were found to ensure that some of that prosperity was funnelled back into the war effort.

Soldiers helping to bring in the harvest on a West Fife farm in the first year of the war.

This graphic by a fifth year pupil at Beath High School in 1945 shows the influence of official artists celebrating workers in essential industries.

Within reason people had always chosen where they worked and at what occupation. This changed. The war economy meant that some occupations and some industries could not be undermanned. Military service had taken a valuable part of the work-force away. They had to be replaced, in many cases with conscripted labour. Factories which, before the war, had produced in response to the markets and consumer demand, were now directed strategically. The textile mills of Dunfermline changed to producing parachute silk and tent fabrics, the floor-cover factories of Kirkcaldy switched to armaments and blackout material. Famously the De La Rue works at Leslie, which had manufactured fountain pens, now made shell casings. Ploughshares, it seemed, had now to be beaten back into swords.

But the problem showed itself first on the land. Imported foods were in short supply. There was an urgent need to increase home food

58

production. The only way to do this was to direct labour on to the land. The creation of the Women's Land Army, young women conscripted to work the fields, was the government's answer. In Fife, many young women, who might have expected to start their working lives in offices or shops, found themselves driving tractors and thinning turnips. Many were volunteers:

Elizabeth Gardner was attending Auchterderran High School when war broke out. She volunteered for the Land Army because her mum didn't want her to be too far away. She eventually worked at farms at Inzievar and Clunie and in market gardens in Cairneyhill. She found that she liked the work and, marrying a farmer after the war, it became her life.

Elsa McFarlan of Kilconquar joined the Women's Land Army and got a job two miles from her own village:

It was quite exciting when my uniform was delivered, it consisted of corduroy breeches, cream shirts made of a sort of aertex material, long top socks, tie and a green vee-necked pullover. For outside wear we were given really well-made jackets and a felt hat. For work on the farm we had khaki dungarees and a jacket as well as very good shoes and boots.

But, for all this she had to give up her clothes coupons:

so, at the end of the war we had nothing feminine to wear. As I got married just at the end of the war I'm afraid I had a pretty scrappy lot of clothes to take on honeymoon.

Elsa remembers:

singling beets and turnips, and harvesting. I can remember being in tears on frosty mornings with having to pull beets out of the ground when it was covered in rime!

Betty Healy was working in Dundee when she volunteered for the Land Army. After training in Aberdeen she was placed at Urquhart Farm near Dunfermline where she had to get up at 3 a.m. to bring in the cows, milk them, bottle the milk, have breakfast, then take the horse and cart to deliver the milk. She shared a cottage with four other Land Girls. One week out of four was spent helping in the farmhouse the other three working on the farm. Farmers didn't impress Betty. She remembers when she had to leave the farm to visit her mother who was ill the farmer docked ten shillings off her pay. She remembers being given: 'a quarter of a scone and half a sausage for breakfast!' She worked in this farmer's

Land Army girls on a farm near Wormit. Farmer's wife is in the centre. Rina Pringle from Cowdenbeath at top right.

As an agricultural county Fife benefited greatly from the contribution of the Women's Land Army. Perhaps the majority of the Land Girls were local but for most of them this was their first experience of life on the farm.

By this personal message I wish to express to you

BETSY GRIEVE

my appreciation of your loyal and devoted service as a member of the Women's Land Army from 22nd July, 1942 to 1st January, 1946. Your unsparing efforts at a time when the victory of our cause depended on the utmost use of the resources of our land have earned for you the country's gratitude.

Elizabeth R

fields until the sixth month of her pregnancy. Just before she left she was asked to plant two fields of potatoes. Possibly Betty was not the anonymous Land Girl quoted in the *Fife Free Press* in September 1943 who said, apparently:

> Sore backs disappear when your heart is in the job. To fight in the battle-line of production is as great an adventure as bringing home a convoy.

Betty's contribution to the war effort continued after leaving the Land Army but now with the WVS with whom she had a long and distinguished association.

Another area of work which relied heavily on conscripted labour was the coal industry. Pressure on coal production was continuous throughout the war. Yet a severe manpower shortage set in almost from the beginning. At the start of hostilities many young, fit miners were members of the Territorial Army. They were immediately called up. Many more volunteered. In 1943, the Minister of Labour, Ernest Bevin introduced a scheme by which ten per cent of men conscripted for service would be directed into the mines. And so were created the famous Bevin Boys whose Scottish recruits received their initial training at Muircockhall in Townhill, Dunfermline. Muircockhall was an antiquated working which had been put on a 'care and maintenance' basis. Though no coal was produced its main shaft, cage and ventilation were in working order. Each Bevin Boy received a few weeks' introduction to the workings of a pit, and some physical fitness training before being deployed to a working pit.

Pressure on coal output was continuous throughout the war and beyond. Here the record breaking shift at Kelty's Benarty Mine in 1945 look fairly nonchalant about their achievement.

Bill Ingram came from a farming background in the Fraserburgh area and knew nothing about the industry before he was called up: 'we had a coal fire but I never thought where it had come from'. He spent four weeks at Muircockhall doing PT, handling hutches, learning safety routines before being sent to Lumphinnans No 11 where he stayed at a hostel in Cowdenbeath. At the pit his first job was:

> what you call a wood-boy, I carried the wood up to the coalface . . . it was a wee splint and it was two feet high . . . as time went on you seemed to get a better job like, which was much safer than that besides, I didn't like the coalface at all like, there was very few Bevin Boys working at the coalface. You got a job as a wood-boy, but never worked on the coalface, very few.

Bill Hart was a Glaswegian who had worked for a telephone rental company. Eventually he found himself at the Michael where he started at the picking tables:

> There were a lot of women there but you couldn't see them, because all you saw were their eyes. They were all covered up with old clothes, you know covered in dust . . . you were on these picking tables, sometimes you picked out the stones, other times you picked out the coal. I think that was just to break us in really . . . when you went down the Michael, the Michael was a fairly modern

pit you know and when you went underground there and you got to the bottom it was about, I think it was about 200 fathoms that one. Anyway when you went down there it was huge, just like Dundee High Street when you went down! All the crates and tubs full of coal and the men walking about all wrapped up as it was very cold down there with the air drafts.

Bill found himself getting along reasonably well with his workmates:

They were all right, I found them all right. They were rough and they cursed and they swore and they told horrible jokes the same as anybody else and they drank a lot . . . when they realised you could work as hard as they could work, I mean if they could shovel coal, I could shovel coal . . . it was hard going. We were only oncost workers, I think it was only a pound a day we got and you got an extra pound if you worked five shifts so you got £6. And if you worked four shifts you only got £4 so it was as well to work the other shifts.

Jim Mackie remembered the Bevin Boys he had working beside him in the Mary Pit:

We had about eight guys, that I can remember, they were people from the cities and that, never been down pits . . . they were at a hostel at Kelty Junction . . . they soon swung into the thing, it was surprising how they adjusted. But again you always got the bad tattie in the bag. So they would lie in the hostel and they wouldn't go to their work. So the next thing they were arrested and they took them to the court and they were fined.

In fact, it was not only Bevin Boys who could appear before the courts. Absenteeism was an offence in all the essential industries. Bus drivers, factory workers etc could all face sheriff court fines if they were absent from work without a good enough reason. In general, this discipline was accepted by most as allowable – at least in wartime.

Jim remembers the women at the screening plant as well:

I started at the tables where you picked the stones out of the coal. And I got a surprise for there were six women. Because that was usually the first job for the boys, get them on the surface screening plants and things like that. They were there about two to two and a half year, then they heard about better jobs at Lathalmond and Rosyth and so, instead of having a dirty job they got a clean job then.

It may have been cleaner but you could still pay a price. Mrs Mcghie recalls:

> I worked at the Naval Stores Depot at Lathalmond: it was a big place then, lots of people working there including Italian POWs. There was everything there and the drivers used to come up from the Dockyard to load up. My job was to pack incendiary devices, they came down a chute one by one. I caught them and packed them in boxes. That's how I have trouble with my ears. I caught a shell and it went off in my hand. I woke up in the ambulance on the way to the West Fife Hospital. It was a very rare thing. I was just unlucky.

'Women's work' in Fife has rarely been of a light nature. And war did not change this for the better. Jean Roberts of Kirkcaldy was conscripted from her job in the Co-op drapery to work in SHEPRO (shell production) in Barry, Ostlere and Shepherd's Works in Kirkcaldy:

> There were two shifts, 6 a.m. to 2 p.m., 2 p.m. to 10 p.m. and a six day week. [she was paid £2 10s a week – which was less than munitions workers were paid – as she was classed as a linoleum worker, although the work actually consisted of making and reconditioning shell casings!] The work was unpleasant, the smell of paint and chemicals caused a lot of people to faint. It was very noisy and the metal parts very heavy. Everyone wore gloves to protect their hands from metal splinters.

Munitions workers at Barry, Ostlere and Shepherd's factory in Kirkcaldy. There is no explanation why one of the women photographed here is not wearing a boiler suit like the others. Perhaps she was really a secretary?

After the war the factory went back to linoleum production.

Munitions and war production brought special hazards. Jean McCallum's father was a miner but worked for a spell at the Dope Shop at Donibristle Air Station.

> The stuff they used was toxic. The men who worked in the Dope shop got a pint of milk each day. [The belief was that the milk would coat the worker's throat and protect against irritation.]

One woman recalled working in the munitions factory at Crombie making ammunition and explosives. Some of the jobs used to turn her skin yellow which she put down to handling the gunpowder. But the wages were very good . . .

Jean Mclean lived in Kirkcaldy during the war. In 1941 at the age of seventeen she went to work in the De La Rue factory, making bullets, shells, and rivets for aeroplanes. Small and slightly built she remembers everyone laughing at her in her oversize boiler suit – and having to stand on a box to reach the machinery. The shifts were 7 a.m. to 4 p.m., 3 p.m. to 11 p.m. and 11 p.m. to 7 p.m. She remembers it as a happy place however:

> singing along to workers' playtime. But they were so tired at the end of a shift that they had very little social life – although they did go dancing occasionally.

Chrissie Scott of Lochgelly also worked at De La Rue's:

> we made bullet cases and moulded bakelite casings that wires went through. They were used in planes. My job was to bore the holes into the bakelite. We worked three shifts. Some girls had to walk from Dundonald to the war memorial in Bowhill to get the bus to work. Once it got to Leslie we had a field to walk through to get to the factory. When the bus arrived with the nightshift the folks finishing backshift had to run through that field to the bus or it left without you! Backshift finished at ten and the bus got us back for eleven, but we then had a walk from the bus to get to our homes . . . unless it was Friday night! We loved going to the dancing. Friday night after the backshift we got off the bus and went straight to the Town Hall for dancing until 2 a.m. If we were on a dayshift, and were working on the Saturday morning our mother's rule was that if you stayed out until 2 a.m. you still got up for that bus at 5 a.m.

Ina McIntosh worked in the silk factory in Dunfermline:

On top of their shift factory workers took their turn at the rota of firewatching. This picture shows firewatchers at the Castleblair textile factory in Dunfermline.
Back: Willie Laughlan, Bella Condie, Ina Ritchie, Betty Hunter, Sandy Bowman
Front: Annie Jordan and Chrissie Laughlan

Firewatching was a tedious but necessary activity. This picture shows firewatchers taking a break from full alert status at an unknown Dunfermline location.

We wove material from pure silk imported from Switzerland. The material went to be made into parachutes. We also made black ties and pure silk scarves for the forces. When the war broke out we stopped getting the silk and had to get nylon from America instead. When it arrived it looked like bottles of milk. This was wound on to bobbins and then wound on to pirns for weaving.

During the war I was in a team of fire-watchers at the Castleblair Works. We went on duty once a week and were trained to put out fires caused by incendiary bombs. In the summer evenings we trained outside. We were to lie down flat and go to the fire spraying water. Buckets of water stood at intervals along the factory floors, each with a stirrup pump that clipped onto the bucket. There were ten teams of fire-watchers for our factory. If it was our night on duty we got to finish early from work, go home to change clothes and have something to eat, before coming back. We would be on duty from 5 p.m. until 8 a.m The cellar was our recreation room. Sometimes visitors would call in to play dominoes or cards, or just to have a smoke or a blether. The bedrooms: one for the girls, one for the men, were upstairs and there was always a lookout on the roof. If the siren went the men went up to watch, in case we were needed with our buckets. Our team consisted of old men and young women – no hanky panky!

Fire-watching made night-owls of everybody. May Edmondson of Kirkcaldy started work in the Central Library in November 1941, when Miss MacBean was the librarian:

The hours were changed during the war but when I was a fire-watcher, they were 10 a.m. to 7.30 p.m. The library had stirrup pumps and buckets of sand standing by in case of fire, but I don't remember ever being on duty when the siren went. I was a fire-watcher every eighth day. You had to stay all night in the library, from closing time to early morning and you would get home about 8 a.m. However you didn't have to start work until 10 a.m.!

Work, then as now, could be boring. Sarah Mackie of Markinch spent three years of her life at that most depressing of military institutions – the transit camp. HMS *Waxwing*, despite its attractive name, was an unlovely collection of Nissen Huts near Townhill, in Dunfermline. It was a Fleet Air Arm transit camp with a staff, mainly clerical, of about 100 Wrens. Life consisted of eating, working, sleeping and (at the weekend) dancing in these Nissen Huts. To add to the misery the food was grisly. Tea, cabbage and baked beans featured a lot but most hated was Sunday supper: cheese and onions (on dancing night!)

Betty Simpson and friend show off the
decontamination gear in the laundry where
they worked. They seem to find their outfits
hilarious rather than alluring.

A not entirely unstaged picture of sailors and soldiers receiving
volunteer-supplied refreshment at one of Fife's emergency hospitals at
Bennachie in Dunfermline.

Methil Home Guard
in 1939.

The Home Guard on parade at Townhill Church early in 1940.

Home Guard unit in Kinglassie. A curious mixture of postures here: grim-faced military correctness and good humoured nonchalance.

Home Guard units took a pride in their developing role and took on many of the trappings of regular military units. This photograph shows the pipe band formed from members of B company (Benarty).
Top Row l–r: Sam Ferns, George Lowe, George Innes, Barney Clarke, Jimmy MacPherson
Middle: Bert Ganley, Duncan Thomson, Alec Thomson
Front: Jimmy Dunn, Pipe Major Alex Thoms, Lt Charlie Taylor, Maj Will Hunter, Drum Major Jim Mackie, Boy Drummer Jim Mackie

In their early days lacking training, proper uniforms, and equipped with broom handles and sporting weapons, Home Guard units may not have felt able to mount a strenuous defence against enemy action. As the war progressed, proper equipment, transport and (mostly) modern weapons enabled them to provide an effective contribution to the military authorities – taking part in joint exercises, manning road blocks etc.
This photograph shows the officers and NCOs of B company (Benarty).
Top l–r: Lt Pratt, Lt Sandy Brown, Lt Bob Evans, Sgt Major John 'Gunner' Hunter
Bottom l–r: Not known, Captain Scott, Major Will Hunter, Lt Charlie Taylor

Men who volunteered for Home Guard duties found themselves working crazy hours: Annie Newey's father worked on the railway but did regular night patrols from Pettycur Bay to Aberdour. Bob Morris formed part of the Coastal Watch in the St Andrews/ Boarhills area. In the early mornings he manned the Kinkell observation point with seven local farmers and one rifle. Esther Renfrew was 23 when the War started. She was the secretary to the manager of the sugar beet factory in Cupar. Having a reserved occupation meant that she was expected to do voluntary work as well and she found herself doing shifts at the telephone exchange in County Buildings.

Ray Halford of Cupar seems to have been content with a very modest start to working life:

> I started work at 14 just before the end of the war. I got nineteen shillings a week and I gave my mother 7s 6d and paid for my own shorthand lessons which were 5s a week and I had 5 shillings to myself. And you got into the cinema, and your sweeties and your stockings and if you saved up you got a wee trip to Dundee on the Ferry.

And if hours were long, pay was nothing to write home about, and pleasures were simple and innocent, there was, occasionally, the prospect of romance. Ann Lee of Glenrothes worked as a bus conductress based at Kirkcaldy garage:

> I met my husband on the buses. He was from Sheffield in the Royal Engineers. He was billeted in Falkland House and he was on his way back from the pictures. It was the last bus [10.20 p.m.] on Saturday night. He asked me if he wrote to me would I reply. I said I would think about it. I received a letter on the Monday and we continued to write for over a year before we saw each other again. We were married in 1945 for 55 years.

Wood-Engravings by H. M. and Polish Forces.

All Saints Church, St Andrews, by Wlodzimierz Klocek.

Strangers in our Midst

One way to judge a society is to observe how it behaves towards outsiders. It is always unsettling when a community finds itself shaken up a little by incomers. War brings movement of people. Not much of that movement is voluntary. As Fifers dispersed around the world on active service, groups of outsiders came to Fife to work or live in or alongside our own communities. The circumstances of war obliged many of us to get used to rubbing shoulders with people with whom we had not grown up and who had not been our friends and neighbours all our lives: servicemen from overseas and other parts of Britain, conscripted labour, evacuees, prisoners of war, and others.

One of the most prominent groups who lived in Fife during the war was the contingent of Free Polish servicemen. They were part of the defence of the eastern coast of Scotland and they lived, were billeted and camped, in almost every part of the county. They were conspicuous by their appearance – in the early days of the Polish presence their uniforms seemed exotic, especially those of the officers – and by their manners, which could seem rather courtly and formal. There was also a great deal of sympathy for their situation as exiles from an occupied country separated, in many cases, from their families and forced to live for who knew how long among strangers. They were also the group who seemed to make most effort to become part of the communities in which they lived. The official policy of their authorities was that they would behave as perfect guests in their temporary homeland. Polish friendship societies were created to foster community and cultural bonds and Polish units formed concert parties which gave entertainments at Christmas or in support of fund raising activities.

In the nature of things the longer that the Poles remained in Fife the increasing informal contacts with the local population created opportunities for friendships, love affairs and marriages which have had

Opposite: **Polish troops were stationed in Fife for a long time. Without the usual army comfort of home leave many Poles made a special effort to become part of the local community. Many were cultured, educated men with artistic interests and talents.**

The Polish Officers are showing their dear friends,

THE SCOTTISH CHILDREN
: OF DUNFERMLINE :

On 30th DECEMBER 1941,

how the folks in Poland were entertained at Christmas
time with a show called

" SZOPKA "

The Show is compiled, produced and managed by
Lt.-Col. Targowski Franciszek

The musical part will be performed by the Polish Army Choir, under the conductorship of
Lt. Kolaczkowski Jerzy

Decorations designed by
Lt. Klebkowski Witold

and executed by him, with the aid of other Polish Officers

Girl dancers' costumes made by the wives of Polish Officers

The part in the show are taken by Polish Officers stationed in Dunfermline and three Scottish girls from Dunfermline :

Margaret Bishop, Queen Anne J.S. School
Jean Pitcher. Ella Chalmers, High School

Dances performed by :
Corp. Rogoyski Jan   Miss Mabel Neil

4 Scottish Girls from Dunfermline :

Nessie Balfour, Queen Anne J.S. School
Betty Hemsworth, Queen Anne J.S. School
Mary Kyle, Queen Anne J.S. School
Annie Young, Queen Anne J.S. School

and 4 Scottish girls from
Miss Mabel Neil's Children's School of Dancing, Glasgow :

Margaret Addie   Mary Friel
Jeananne Hendry   Ellen Kenny

Polish forces, during their long stay in Fife, made a real contribution to the life of the community. Their concerts, for both children and adults, were very popular.

POCZTÓWKA—POST CARD

THE POLISH NATIONAL ANTHEM.

"JESZCZE POLSKA NIE ZGINELA."

POLAND IS NOT YET LOST.

" While we live she is existing,
Poland is not fallen;
We will win with swords resisting,
What the foe has stolen,
March, march, Dabrowski.
From Italy's plain;
Our Brethren shall meet us
In Poland again."

Souvenir from

"Szopka Polska"

(The Polish Christmas Pantomime)

arranged by Polish Soldiers
for School Children
in Dunfermline.

With Best Wishes
for a Happy New Year.

30th December 1941.

dojdziemy!

At midday, every day for hundreds of years, a trumpet call sounded from the famous tower of St Mary's Church in Cracow, but when the German hordes overran Poland they tried to stamp out every Polish custom. So they silenced the trumpet.

But at mid-day every day, though hundreds of miles from Poland, the trumpet still sounds the Cracow call. It rings out from the four windows of a tower in a Scottish country town and reminds our Allies of our common aim to defeat the enemy and restore the ancient customs of Poland and other lands.

By happy coincidence two towers are adjacent in that Scottish country town, and in their humble way they bear some slight resemblance to the twin towers of Cracow.

The artist, in designing the Christmas Card shown here, suggests how the call carries the thoughts of the Polish soldier to his own beloved land; and that the day of his return is approaching is conveyed by the word "Dojdziemy"—"we are on the road".

Cupar formed a very special relationship with its Polish forces.
From the *Fife News Almanac 1942*

a permanent effect on our community. As Jim Douglas puts it in his reminiscence of wartime Kelty:

> The Poles had a way with women, especially the officers. The clicking heels and perfect manners, worlds apart from 'can ah see ye hame hen?' or 'Di yi fancy a pudden supper?' Fights broke out at the local dance halls. Several of the soldiers married local girls, stayed on after the war and integrated well into the community, most being hard working, resourceful men, willing to attempt a variety of jobs.

The picture of the suave, lady-killing Pole has almost become a legend in Fife's collective memory but there is no mistaking the admiration which the young and possibly impressionable May Edmondson felt for the:

> Colonel who lived in Sang Road and came into the library, wearing his cape. He and his wife were very smart. He would click his heels and bow when he was returning his books.

Sadly, heel clicking and bowing has not become a feature of the behaviour of Fife's library patrons.

Ray Halford has another kind of memory, that of patriotic Poles who were determined to keep thoughts of their homeland uppermost:

> And then of course through the War we had the Polish soldiers, a lot of them. When the Polish soldiers came, those from Cracow, and they saw the Corn Exchange, and its tower was so like their tower in Cracow so every day at 12 o'clock there were two buglers and they took turn about at playing the bugle from the four sides and this was to keep their memories [of their homeland].

This ceremony at the corn exchange in Cupar came to be regarded with affection by the people of Cupar as they became more attached to their Polish guests.

Janet Harper of Auchtermuchty lived in Leven during the War and remembers:

> We had a Russian girl that married on one of our soldiers, and I've often wondered, since I don't live in Leven, what happened to her, she was a lovely looking girl . . . plenty of Polish soldiers that stayed on in Leven and a lot of my friends that stayed around me married Polish soldiers . . .

Ray O'Riardon, who stayed in St Andrews, recalled that:

on the whole we were very pro the Poles and they had beautiful manners and were lovely dancers. There were a lot of dances . . . there was the café in St Andrews and the Victoria Café and MacArthur's had a lovely big room at the back and that was where they had dances.

Mrs Milczynska remembers the Polish soldiers coming to Cupar in the Autumn of 1940. She was sixteen at the time:

They used to make trinkets from aluminium castings, primarily their national emblem the white eagle. They were very patriotic and staunchly Roman Catholic.

Later, in 1951 she married a Pole who had been evacuated at Dunkirk but was given a medical discharge at Cupar. Sunday school halls, the Guide Hall, and the Royal Hotel were all used as billets. What is now the Cairnie Fruit farm was once the Polish hospital.

Esther Renfrew, also of Cupar, remembers that local families were asked to billet Polish officers. Neighbours across the street were asked to billet their Chief Chaplain, Father Tomczak who was a great friend of General Sikorski. He often used to obtain Nivea Cream from the NAAFI for Esther and her family on his visits to Edinburgh.

Esther often goes to see Our Lady at Falkland Palace which the Polish soldiers made out of corned beef tins and shell casings. It seems right that there should be permanent reminders of the Polish presence in Fife. Although everyone has memories of superficial things – like their use of talcum powder and cologne, a sophistication too far for the men of 1940s Scotland – ultimately their story is a poignant one. Most of them never returned to their homeland and many of them remained in Fife. In doing so the national identity they were so proud of in the war years has become diluted and they have become absorbed into our own community.

Another group whose stay was to have an impact on Fife were the Prisoners-of-War. Their status as 'guest' was not quite the same as that of the Poles but they too have left memories embedded with us that are, perhaps surprisingly, rather positive. Jim Douglas again:

Picture is of a Sicilian POW who worked at Newtonhall farm for three years of the war. He kept in touch after his return to Italy.

We worked with Italian prisoners of war at the tattie-howkin, sad, sallow, dark-eyed men, wistfully showing us crumpled photographs of their families. They were kind and considerate, enjoying the company of children as substitutes for their own, pointing at the snapshots then at us, indicating that we were roughly the same age.

They were utilised as labour, mainly on the farms and, as the war progressed became part of the scenery in many rural parts of Fife. To Jim Douglas the amount of freedom they had seemed astonishing:

Their camp was situated near my granny's house at Black Dub and our lorry picked them up in the morning and dropped them off at night.

They were often unaccompanied by guards. Ray Halford recalls:

There was a big camp out at Ladybank, a POW camp, I think they were mostly Italians, a few Germans but mainly Italians and it got towards the end of the war they were allowed out and about and we couldn't get into the cinemas for them!

Janet Scott of Cowdenbeath remembered:

the Italian POWs billeted at Thomson's Farm, just by Beath Church. I had a bracelet made by them out of silver thruppenny bits, I think they made things like that to make a wee bit of money.

There seemed to be something of a live-and-let-live attitude to prisoners: a realisation that they were really just ordinary people like themselves. There was very little of the aura of 'the enemy' about them. Elsa McFarlan remembers working alongside them on farms when she was in the Land Army:

We had German POWs who came in lorries. They were just used at the busy times. We also had Italian prisoners and the Germans disliked them saying they

Prisoner of War labour became a significant contribution to work on the farm. Over time the close working relationship between farmer and worker overcame many of the barriers which naturally existed between prisoners and their 'hosts'. This picture shows Fritz and Rudi, German POWs at Newtonhall Farm.

were lazy and dirty. As I could speak a bit of German I learned that they were just like our own men, caught up in a war not of their making. They had photos of their wives and girlfriends just like soldiers anywhere. However there was one who the others shunned and he just had a picture of himself in a Nazi uniform!

Alex McArthur lived in Kinglassie during the war:

I worked on Goatmilk Farm and we had two German Prisoners-of-War working for us. They had a camp just outside Kinglassie and the POWs were distributed to work across the local area on the farms. We used to ask them why they didn't try to escape and they said they were happy to stay where they were. They used to say [perhaps a little tongue-in cheek, this] this was just like a hotel they were treated so well. The farmers used to really look after them.

Not all Italians in Fife were prisoners. Most towns and villages had one or two families of Italian background. Many had been here since the beginning of the century. Most ran catering businesses: cafes, ice-cream and chip shops. By and large they were a settled part of the community and most accepted them as such. With the coming of war with Germany there were some rumblings about the loyalty of a national group whose homeland, it was felt, would soon enter the conflict on the side of Hitler. A curious mixture of motives seems to animate the following [anonymous] letter-writer in 1940:

... many of them of long standing here are not naturalised, doubtless for some sinister purpose. Our shopkeepers have to suffer unfair competition from them as their premises are open until far into the night and morning. The profits from fish, chips, tobacco, ice-cream etc must be enormous and it is to be hoped that the profits are bearing their proper share of taxation ... hanging about their foreign shops by our young to all hours of the night is not for their good. I am &c Scotia.

But, of course, hanging about their foreign shops was just what the youth of Fife liked to do!

Scotia was no doubt pleased by the actions of the authorities in the next few days. As soon as Italy had declared war the police moved into action rounding up and interning Italian nationals. In Kirkcaldy, as reported in the *Fife Free Press*,

The round-up was accomplished by police officers in cars, and so quietly and so unobtrusively was it carried out that very few members of the public were aware that it had been done.

The policy, as it turned out, was not one that the government was to take much pride in. It produced the anomaly of some families having sons on active service with the British army while the grandparents were being interned in camps. With the population in general the policy seemed not to be popular. There was an isolated stoning of a shop window in Kirkcaldy but otherwise the Italian families received much sympathy. Mr Wilkie of Cowdenbeath recalled:

The local Italian families were interned during the war, in case they were a threat. Didn't seem fair. We all knew them.

Janet Harper was even more indignant:

One of the injustices in Leven was, we had the Dorianos, they were Italian, they had the fish and chip shop and the ice cream shop and so on and they were interned during the war. And they were part of our community. They had been there longer than I had . . . they were our friends.

And what of those other incomers, the Bevin Boys? What kind of reception did they have? In a way the Bevin Boys were not unlike the prisoners of war! They lived in camps or hostels. They mixed with the local population mainly in the workplace. And, finally, they were here, not because they wanted to be, but because they had no choice. A few Bevin Boys took to the life, married local girls and stayed on at the pits after their compulsory service was over. By far the majority served their time then returned at once to rebuild their lives and careers. Most former Bevin Boys have some mixed feelings about their time in the pit and their lives in the Fife mining communities: on the one hand they recognised that there was a special comradeship in the mine and that those who worked underground had developed a special ethos of togetherness and taking care of those around them but, on the other hand, they felt that there was always something of a barrier between them and those who had been born and raised to a life in the industry.

David M Nicoll was an engineering apprentice in Arbroath when he was called up and eventually found himself working in the pits in the Cowdenbeath area. He stayed in a group of Nissen huts where the Bevin Boys slept, ate, washed, and, to a large extent, passed the time:

. . . one of the rooms was set aside for some dancing and we had a dance on Tuesday nights . . . when I got to know some of the chaps

I was working with, we met some of the miners underground, 'oh Bevin Boy, you'll get nothing up there, she's no giving you that dance on Tuesday night'. That was very reminiscent of what I heard before I went there, because in Arbroath, when Poland was overrun, there was a lot of Pole soldiers billeted in Arbroath and it was the same thing . . . there was dances laid on, you know, and I heard our mothers, 'You're no dancing with the Poles' and I was in the situation, 'You're no getting dancing with they Bevin Boys up there.'

Bob Wilson worked in a bank in Aberdeen and first worked as a Bevin Boy at the Michael in East Wemyss:

You were never one of them. There was one of the safety men, the deputy safety man where I was working, he came from mining stock himself and this is a miner but he had been twenty five years in East Wemyss and he still wasn't one of them . . . I don't think it was just a Fife thing . . . some of the fishing villages in the North East . . . but there was no hostility or anything like that. The majority of us settled in . . . there were one or two conscientious objectors, older blokes, but they were never treated any different.

John Ritchie was an electrical engineering apprentice and also ended up at the Michael. His first impression on going underground was quite good:

The miners were really helpful and good and one of the things that aye makes me laugh, you were all right on the main road where you were walking but when you went down to the other sections it was smaller roads and all that you would hear would be 'mind your feet' 'watch your head' and this was because if there was anything you might trip over you only had your wee lanterns you see.

In the end there was really a slightly wary acceptance of each other. The miners could respect that the Bevin Boy might come from a different background from them but were adapting to a situation they had never asked to be in. Jim Mackie:

And I can mind some. They were well off and well spoken . . . it was surprising how they adjusted . . . it was an experience for them. Some of them were farmers – they were good workers. The Bevin Boys were quite adaptable – it was surprising how they adapted, given the different situations.

So, there were worse places to find yourself a stranger than in Fife. The County had always been seen as slightly isolated with tight little communities of farmers, weavers, miners and fishermen. But, on the whole the people adapted well to the influx of foreigners and strangers. As young Fife men and women went abroad and extended their horizons it was probably healthy that life at home was given a bit of a shake up.

Esther Renfrew remembers her parents in Cupar as being rather conservative in their attitudes. She herself, at the age of twenty three, had to be home by 9.30 p.m. in the evening while any escort who accompanied her home was sent packing by her father. In the meantime three of her brothers had joined the Royal Air Force and a sister had enrolled in the WAAFs. She still remembers her mother's outrage when a son returned home with an *English* girlfriend. Her outrage was doubled when she discovered that she was in the habit of wearing *trousers!* Esther was pleased to be able to relate that her mother was completely won round and formed a special closeness with this exotic addition to her family.

CITY AND ROYAL BURGH OF DUNFERMLINE.

CIVIL DEFENCE.

To Members of the Civil Defence General Services.

On the occasion of the cessation of hostilities in Europe and the "standing down" of the Civil Defence Services I wish, on behalf of the Magistrates, Councillors and Citizens of Dunfermline, to thank you for your loyal devotion to duty during the critical years which have just passed.

At the beginning of the war, Dunfermline was rated very high as a vulnerable point and it is to the credit of all who joined the Civil Defence Services that so efficient an Organisation was formed, ready to deal with any emergency that might arise.

Although we have not altogether escaped unscathed, we have indeed been fortunate to have been spared heavy air attacks.

Few will forget the memorable days, especially in 1940 and 1941, when "alerts" were of frequent occurrence, and the knowledge that a highly trained body of men and women were standing by ready to give assistance should the necessity arise, had, I am certain, a very steadying effect on the morale of the population.

I wish to thank you most heartily for the services you have rendered and wish you the best of luck for the future.

[signature]

Provost.

City Chambers,
Dunfermline.

28th May, 1945.

An Ending?

Many of the features of life in Fife during the war didn't end in 1945. Of course there was the freedom from some of the anxieties of wartime. The threat of any kind of direct attack on Fife from the air or from the sea had receded long ago. And now there was more or less an end to fears for the safety of family members serving abroad. Blackout restrictions were now at an end but, in effect, there had been a relaxation in the strictness of the regulations for some time. Some of the miseries of the war period, of course, didn't end at all. Rationing was still in place and, with the economic crisis of the post war years, was set to continue for some time. Morgan Neale, after nine years of rationing in Dunfermline flew out to Malta with his mother in 1949. At his medical inspection on arrival the doctor's pronouncement was 'perfectly fit, slightly malnourished, *as expected*'.

Weddings, of which there were many in 1945 and 1946, still required ingenuity and planning to put on any kind of a show. Elma Cheetham remembers:

> When I was married in 1945 I was a 'borrowed bride!' my dress came all the way from South Africa, loaned by a cousin of my mother, my veil by an aunt, and the white satin shoes by the daughter of a friend of my mother-in-law . . . the dress arrived safely in a box marked 'used clothing'.

For many the end of the war was of course a time for celebration. But in many parts of Fife the celebration seemed rather muted, dutiful rather than spontaneous. The *East Fife Observer* reported Anstruther's celebration thus:

> On the whole the first of the VJ holidays in this area was celebrated very quietly. Flags and bunting appeared very slowly, but

Opposite: **With the ending of hostilities the civil defence organisations 'stood down'. They deserved their praise if only for the tremendous number of hours put in to what were – largely – unrewarding tasks.**

ultimately quite a brave show was made. A Victory dance was held in Anstruther Town Hall in the evening. A united service of thanksgiving is to be held in Chalmers Memorial Church on Sunday evening.

This was Anstruther's wild response to the criticism it had received for its poor showing three months earlier on VE Day.

May we through the medium of your paper say how annoyed we were about no VE day celebrations. It most certainly showed up the slowness of our Provost and Town Councillors. There was no excuse for it whatever. We have a fine Town Hall in Anstruther but it was closed against ratepayers who would have liked to have shown a patriotic spirit, and where was its flag? We saw this great day coming, but seemingly no preparations were made the result being we had to make the most of VE day in the sale ring.

If Anstruther knew what a good time was but preferred, on the whole, not to have it, then there was a little more enthusiasm in other parts of Fife.

After Mr Attlee's broadcast, Kirkcaldy suddenly came alive. Ship's sirens set up a wailing note from the Forth, the noise of the fireworks increased and revellers started to walk through the streets singing and cheering. Thus, those who had gone to bed were not long left unaware that there was something big afoot, especially as a bell started to toll between 12 and 1. Bonfires were lit in various parts of the town, many of them in the middle of streets, and impromptu dances were held.

The *Fife Free Press* reported the spontaneous revelry of VJ night but also described the more restrained activities of the following day with approval:

There was no sign of the over-exuberance which has marred festivities in some quarters of the globe and a good time was had without the peace being unduly disturbed.

VE Day (Victory in Europe) was announced on 8 May 1945. VJ Day (Victory over Japan) was announced at midnight on Tuesday 14 August 1945. On both occasions there was a public holiday, two days in the case of the VJ celebrations.

Norman Cunningham remembers the VE day parade in Leven, which also produced one of the last casualties of aerial bombardment of the war:

Highlight was the envelopes dropped from an aeroplane flying over the parade route. I didn't get one but there was a few souvenirs in each one. A young boy was hit on the head by one of the envelope bags accidentally dropped from the plane and I believe the pilot and some of his crew visited him in hospital.

But not the last casualty of all. Tom Pearson of Newburgh was only six when the war ended but can remember a bonfire in the town where an effigy of Hitler was burned. A drunk man became too enthusiastic bombarding the effigy and fell in the flames. He had to be extinguished by the firefighters.

But, all in all the tone of the end of the war was set more by the reception given to returning prisoners. Many have memories of these scenes – even those who had no direct connection with the returnees. Ruth Brown of Kirkcaldy recalls the ex prisoners of the Japanese coming home. Her mother's ex fiance was one of the returning prisoners who stepped off the train and she remembers her mother crying when she saw his condition. John Gow of Ladybank remembers:

the POWs coming back home. There was a big street party for them. One at the Rossend district and one in Somerville Street. This was really something. I remember some being shaky and debilitated.

In a way it was strange that the actual celebrations at the end of the war were so restrained. One thing that seems apparent is that the war years were when Fifers learned to enjoy themselves. The very early decision to close almost everything down was soon reversed. There was an appetite for entertainment. The cinemas were full. Despite stern resistance by local clergymen the Sunday opening of cinemas in Dunfermline was obtained as a result of pressure from Forces welfare officers. All kinds of spectator sport thrived, from football to ice hockey. In the immediate post war years greyhound racing and speedway were added. But the biggest draw of all was dancing. Young people, especially women, couldn't get enough of it. In many ways this was the group which experienced the most radical change in the period. Independence and hard working

1939————————————————1945

On behalf of the People of the Burgh of Leven and the Parish of Scoonie, the Committee take this opportunity of expressing to you their Grateful Thanks for and Deep Appreciation of Honoured Service rendered to the Nation in the Cause of Freedom, and offer you their Deepest Sympathy in the Loss of Your Dear One

Greater love hath no man than this
That he lay down his life for his friends

1939————————————————1945

Official Condolence Card

lives gave many of them the feeling that it was their right to have an evening's entertainment on their own terms. And they went for it. Jessie Herd of Leven remembers being: 'danced of her feet by sailors in the Jubilee Hall'. May Edmondson recalls that:

> all the big bands came to Kirkcaldy's Ice Rink. A third of the rink area was made into a dance floor and you could hear bands like Joe Loss, Geraldo and the Squadronaires. The resident band was Simon Stungo's.

May remembers his signature tune to this day but can't put a name to it.

Men, especially middle aged fathers, were rather left behind. Mrs Milczynska remembers that her mother wanted to work in the County Buildings in Cupar as part of the war effort but her father refused. He thought, 'it was not the done thing for married women to go out and work'. In the same way her father at first would not let her go dancing or walk down the Bonnygate on her own on a Sunday. 'Only common girls did that.' Eventually her mother was allowed to work in communications at Haymount on a part-time basis.

Jean Thomson of East Wemyss was twelve when the war started. She

Many organisations held delayed victory celebrations. This programme was for the anniversary celebration held by Hay and Robertson, textile manufacturers in Dunfermline.

HAY & ROBERTSON LTD.
ST. MARGARET'S WORKS
DUNFERMLINE

Victory
Social and Dance

7 p.m.

Friday   Elgin St. Hall
7th June 1946   Dunfermline

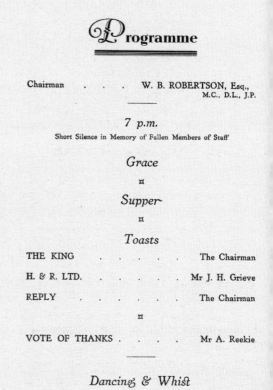

𝒫rogramme

Chairman . . . W. B. ROBERTSON, Esq.,
M.C., D.L., J.P.

7 p.m.
Short Silence in Memory of Fallen Members of Staff

Grace

¤

Supper

¤

Toasts

THE KING . . . . . The Chairman

H. & R. LTD. . . . . Mr J. H. Grieve

REPLY . . . . . The Chairman

¤

VOTE OF THANKS . . . Mr A. Reekie

Dancing & Whist

played piano accordion in a concert party run by Jean Hunter. They used to play all over Fife. She remembers being ferried over to Inchcolm to entertain the garrison. One soldier taught her to play billiards. 'Father would not have been happy if he had found out.'

Frank Melville worked in Rosyth Dockyard during the war. Dancing and nightlife were very important to the young people among his workmates. He remembers a kind of social hierarchy among dance venues. Lowest was the snake-pit in Rosyth. Then Dunfermline Co-op. At the top, for the most elegant dancing, was the Kinema Ballroom.

Thomas Foster was sixteen when the war started and worked in Fordell Pit with other local men. But things began to look up with the arrival of newcomers:

> The Poles and the Italians made a difference to the social life. They organised dances and we all went. They were right natty dressers – better than us.

Margaret Green of Auchtermuchty recalls a series of incidents which illustrates very well the social changes which began to affect Fife as the war progressed:

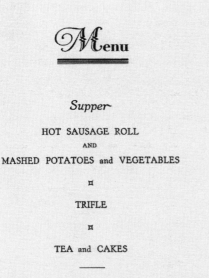

Menu

Supper

HOT SAUSAGE ROLL
AND
MASHED POTATOES and VEGETABLES

¤

TRIFLE

¤

TEA and CAKES

————

God Save The King . . . . 1 a.m.

ICES

TEA - - CAKES - - LEMONADE

A year on from the end of hostilities did not mean that celebrations could be as lavish as the occasion would seem to warrant. As this menu shows, factory workers at Hay and Robertson are invited to feast on sausage rolls and mashed potatoes washed down with tea and – no doubt unlimited – lemonade.

"Dunfermline and West Fife Journal," August 22, 1945.

DUNFE
& WEST FIF

NCORPORATING · DUNFERMLINE JOURNAL

o. 415. [Registered at the G.P.O as a Newspaper.] DUNFERMLINE AND WEST FIFE JO

VJ DAY ARRIVES!

How Dunfermline Rejoiced

ler almost a week of standing by with paradoxically mixed feelings of jubilation and frustration, the hooting of ship's sirens, the shrieking of locomotive whistles, the blaring of musical instruments, the gleam of numerous bonfires, and the blinding glare of searchlights criss-crossing each other as they swept the heavens, told the people of Dunfermline at midnight on Tuesday that the war with Japan had ended in the success of the Allied nations, and that peace had come at last to a war weary world.

Because of the rumours and unter-rumours that were current in the preceding five days regarding the declaration of peace, any citizens had retired for the ght and as a result failed to hear e official broadcast by Mr C. R. tlee, Prime Minister, of the unditional surrender of Japan, hich came at midnight.

There were many thousands, wever, who, with a keener presence of the course of the world-ide drama, awaited with gleeful nticipation the glad tidings, and hen the official announcement as made were ready to commence a victory celebration. The lin ra¹ by the laughing, cheer-g, victory-crazed celebrants soon wakened the sleepers, who, on earning the cause, rapidly left heir beds and, hastily donning utdoor attire, added their quota to the general celebrations.

The centre of Dunfermline's elebrations on Tuesday night was at a huge bonfire erected near the flagstaff at the top of the Public Park. As if by magic less than half-an-hour after the declaration of peace a crowd numbering about

ing the festivities, although on a much smaller scale.

A downpour of rain on Wednesday forenoon put a slight damper on the jubilations, but matters brightened up considerably towards evening when the weather became more favourable. There was public dancing in Pittencrieff Park and the Public Park to the strains of pipe bands and loud speaker vans on Wednesday and Thursday, much to the enjoyment of the younger people whose energy appeared unsatiable.

Townhill and Rosyth provided entertainment for their own inhabitants much on the same lines as that of Dunfermline. Almost every street had its own bonfire, around which the kiddies leaped with glee scarcely understanding what it was all about but equally infected with the spirit of the occasion. Special victory dances were held and to the music of bands, several of which were armed with "weird" instruments, people paraded the streets singing and dancing and firing off rockets and squibs.

There was one section of the

After the we
mill Street,

DUNI
FI

Mr James
Globe") Fitz
producer of t
so familiar
cinema-goers,

MLINE
JOURNAL
). 1840 · WEST FIFE ECHO · *ESTD.* 1900

EDNESDAY, AUGUST 22, 1945.   Yearly Subscription.   TWOPENCE
                              Post Free 13/-

iss May G. Stark, Kinross House, Kinross, and Mr R. L. Richardson, Wood-
e, which took place in Canmore Street Congregational Church, Dunfermline,
on Tuesday.

NE	STOLE FUR COAT	DUNFERMLINE OFFICER MENTIONED
of the nous film gue series lar with Scotland	**To Sleep in Field** The sequel to a burglary at a bungalow at 2 Pitbauchlie Bank, Dunfermline on VJ-night took place in Dunfermline Sherin	Colonel R. H. Robertson, Black Watch (R.H.R.), Dunfermline, has been mentioned in dispatches, while serving in Italy with the Allied Commission. He received his promotion to Colonel in

WORLD PEACE
shares the front page
with a local wedding
as people focus on
the future.

Nancy and I were walking to school, and picked up a friend at her gate. Her mum was kissing this Norwegian soldier. And we looked. Our friend said that's Uncle Olaf, he's going to be my new daddy, and I thought what do you do with two daddies? you know? Well, two or three weeks later it was a French sailor. 'He's from Marseilles, he's going to be my new daddy.' Well I went home and saw my dad at dinner time and I was saying to him what's she going to do with three daddies and I can still see his face yet. Years later I realised that this woman had a wonderful war! My father was kind of Victorian and you were supposed to stick to your own and this was just taking hospitality too far. But Dad couldn't help it. It was just the way he was brought up.

Many people were having to adjust from 'the way they were brought up' as times changed and new experiences were thrust upon them. Olive Brown remembers that her:

brother-in-law was in Jamaica during the war . . . Just after the war ended friends of his stayed with us while on leave. We went dancing at the Kinema Ballroom and got some very strange looks because the boys were coloured.

When the *Courier* reported a routine court case at Cupar Sheriff Court in 1944 the journalist was most taken with the fact that two of the accused:

coloured merchant seamen from the British Honduras [wore] JITTERBUGGING SUITS IN COURT, the jackets of which came well below their knees. They wore white and brown shoes and when they left the dock donned brightly coloured straw hats.

By the end of the war there was certainly some kind of feeling that many things would not go back to what they had been before the war. People had spent five years being told what to do, where to live, what to wear, what to eat. There were straws in the wind. The war seemed to loosen some inhibitions. A young woman charged with stealing coal at Dunfermline Sheriff Court responded that 'she hoped the Germans would drop a bomb on the police station and blow all you bastards to hell'. A Kirkcaldy Sheriff could not accept the 'impudent letter' with which a Bevin Boy pleaded guilty to an absenteeism charge. 'I advise you when you are communicating with public authorities you must adopt a more worthy tone.'

The War had brought far reaching changes to Fife. The people of that generation lived in interesting times. The many sacrifices made, the hard work that was performed, almost without question, and the family separations that were endured seemed to produce at the moment of victory a sensation of exhaustion and loss rather than elation. In 1945 the people of Fife had come through a long ordeal in which their lives had been changed in very fundamental ways: Jessie Smith describes her sombre feelings as she returned to rebuild her life in post war Kelty:

I wasn't home until 1946. You had such an empty feeling you didn't know what was going to happen to you, you had to hunt for work. It was really a bad time for me because I had lost all my friends they were scattered around the country, half the folk you knew at home weren't there. It took a year or so to settle down again.

Fleet Air Arm fighter over Donibristle.

Contributors

The following people have kindly contributed photographs, documents and stories which have been used in this book.

Mr Archbold, Margaret Armit, Mollie Balfour, Alison Baxter,
Cecilia Bennett, Olive Brown, Ruth Brown, Alex Cairns,
Elma Cheetham, Jim Clarke, John Corbett, Mrs Cowan,
Norman Cunningham, Ivor Curran, Mrs Curran, Mrs Deans,
George Docherty, Isabella Dryburgh, May Edmondson, Jane Elder,
Thomas Foster, Margaret Fotheringham, Elizabeth Gardner,
Margaret Garvie, John Gow, Robert Grant, Margaret Green,
Ray Halford, Janet Harper, Bill Hart, Betty Healy, Mr Henderson,
Jean Herd, Winifred Hislop, Mary Howie, Lorna Hunter,
Mrs Hutchison, Bill Ingram, May Jakonska, Margaret Joy, Ann Lee,
Jim Mackie, Sarah Mackie, Jean Maclean, David Mason, Betty Mason,
Alex McArthur, Jean McCallum, Rina MacDonald, Mrs MacDonald,
Bert McEwan, Elsa McFarlan, Mrs Mcghie, Ina McIntosh,
James McIntosh, John McWilliams, James Melville, Mrs Milczynska,
Bob Morris, Morgan Neale, Annie Newey, David M Nicoll,
Ray O'Riordan, Tom Pearson, Esther Renfrew, John Ritchie,
Jean Roberts, Chrissie Scott, Betty Simpson, Jessie Smith,
Jean Thomson, Una White, Mr Wilkie, Bob Wilson